# Echoes

# Echoes

### God Is Always Chasing You.
### Can You Hear His Echoes?

## Jenny Bishop

*Echoes*

Trilogy Christian Publishers A Wholly Owned Subsidary of Trinity Broadcasting Network

2442 Michelle Drive Tustin, CA 92780

For information about special discounts for bulk purchases, please contact Trilogy Christian Publishing.

Trilogy Disclaimer: The views and content expressed in this book are those of the author and may not necessarily reflect the views and doctrine of Trilogy Christian Publishing or the Trinity Broadcasting Network.

Manufactured in the United States of America

10 9 8 7 6 5 4 3 2 1

Library of Congress Cataloging-in-Publication Data is available.

ISBN: 979-8-88738-685-0

E-ISBN: 979-8-88738-686-7

# Echoes

God is always running after you; are you listening for His echoes?

# Dedication

To Shane and my boys. I am so proud of all of you and of our family. My love for you is immeasurable.

Boys, always remember to be strong in the Lord, to pray, and to do what is right, even when it's hard.

Follow God's lead in life no matter what. You will do great things, I already know.

And to the little girl, Jenny Ruth, who felt unloved and unwanted, who felt dirty and ruined.

You have been reborn, baby girl, and you are perfected, loved, and worthy in Jesus' name!

# A Special Note from Jenny

Do not give up. I don't know what you might be facing in your life right now, but what I do know is that you cannot give up. God has a good plan for you and for your life. A plan that you most likely cannot even think up on your own. God loves you. You are unique and gifted, and His promises are for you if you accept Jesus as your Lord and Savior and if you're willing to surrender your life completely to Him and use your authority in Jesus to resist Satan at every turn. Resisting Satan is twofold, using your power and authority in Christ via faith, actions, and words, and also behaving in Christlike ways even throughout the storms of life. Satan won't know what to do with you if you are able to stay joyful and peaceful even in the toughest times.

I pray that the words in this book will breathe life into you, bring hope to you, and bring the excitement into your life that only our good and glorious Father can bring. Life with God is an adventure!

In these pages, I share pieces of my personal life's journey with the Lord, but I also give you the biggest life tips that God taught me that transformed my life. Overcoming abuse, bad choices, anger, disappointment, and shame are no easy tasks on our own, but with God's help, you can live in all that He has finished for you.

May God bless you and keep you. May He make His face shine upon you and be gracious to you, and give you His peace.

Amen.

# Table of Contents

# Prologue

"Do you want to hit me, Jenny?"

"No, Mom, I'm not going to hit you," I replied. As she turned and walked out, I heard my dad coming in through the front door. "Well, I hit her," my mom said. "Good," my dad replied.

When I was about sixteen or seventeen years old, my mother held a gun to her head right in front of me and told me she was going to make me watch.

Of course, at that time, I was convinced it was all my fault that she chose to act that way. I was the worst teenager; I gave her such a hard time; she just couldn't take any more of what I was doing; she had no other choice than to act in this way because nothing else was working. These were some of the continuous things I had heard from her.

Out of the dark hallway came my mom. Screaming at the top of her lungs and waving a belt around. My brother and I ducked and covered as she started in on us with the belt. My dad, well, he just stood there. Don't ask me how long it was; I have no clue. It might have been thirty seconds, or it might have been five minutes. I really don't recall. But does that matter?

It was long enough for the belt buckle to break my hand open and for it to start bleeding.

My dad picked me up and took me to the bathroom. He set me on the counter and started to rinse off my hand. I could tell he was upset, but the words he chose to use were, "Look what you made your mother do."

Do you see a pattern here? Do you see habitual behaviors that are not being influenced by God? Was life this way *all of the time*? No, it wasn't. But does that matter?

# Introduction

I was born in 1978 in Littleton, Colorado. I have one younger brother, who is two years younger than I am and resides in Tennessee.

My husband, Shane, and I married in 2016 and have landed ourselves and our two sons, Alex and Ashton, in a small town outside of Fort Worth, Texas.

We love our home, and we are so grateful that God gave it to us. It is truly a piece of heaven on earth.

My husband, Shane, is the rock of our home and my best friend. Without him cheering me on and encouraging me, I don't know that this book would have come to fruition.

For fun, we like taking family walks and hikes, riding bikes, playing tennis, swimming, playing board games, having Friday night family movie nights, playing sports, and doing activities together. Basically, anything with a ball and competition involved, we are in it to win it! As the earthly parents to our boys, we pray we can raise them to understand God's goodness and love for them and that they will grow to be warriors for Christ.

When I was nine years old, I felt a call on my life to help and serve people; I also felt like someday I would be put on a platform to help many, although I had zero clue of what that meant or how that would come to fruition.

This book shares pieces of my journey, the good, the bad, the awful, and the miraculous.

I pray that when you read this, you don't focus on Jenny or what Jenny has to say but that you would focus on God's goodness, God's heart, and know that what He does for one, He will do for all when we choose Him.

## The Incredible Story of the Title of This Book, Echoes

I was about twenty-two years old, renting an old Victorian-style home on Main Street in Hustonville, Kentucky.

The house had good bones but was a fixer-upper, to say the least. The $300 per month rental payment was about all I could afford. I was working full-time as a receptionist at a company called Tarter Gate at the time (maybe you've heard of them?), and receptionist work really didn't pay that well. Regardless, my parents had helped me try to make the house feel like home. They lived about ten to fifteen minutes up the road and enjoyed having me so close. I had set up my old clunky computer in my "dining room" area and sat down one night to write.

I have always enjoyed writing. God gifted me with the ability to sit down and write beautiful poetry and stories, and I found enjoyment in doing so.

This particular night I had zero clue what I was going to write, but I sat down and started typing out these words.

I had been saved when I was six years old, but let's face it, I had not surrendered my life to Christ at this time in my life, nor did I really even understand what that meant or even that it was something I needed to do. But God was always chasing after me with His plan, and thankfully I didn't argue too much when He put something in my heart to do.

Little did I know that over twenty years later, this poem/song would become a part of this book and would be the title that God told me to use.

I hope you enjoy this poem/song about God's relentless pursuit of each and every one of us.

This old world keeps on turning faster every day

No use in trying to stop it

You just have to go your way

Leave the past behind you; play the cards you've been dealt


But don't you know, it ain't that easy, and have you ever felt


The echoes in the darkness, through those old pine trees

The distant sound of Him every night saying, "Come on back to Me"

The echoes in the mountains, crashing through the snow

Chasing you down that winding road no matter where you go


Can you hear the echoes?


And every day, you battle

Your own thoughts and every words

You smile, and you laugh, but oh, how much it hurts


And you can feel His soft whisper gently brush across your cheek

And you can feel His subtle breath blow right through you when you sleep

Oh, the echoes in the darkness, through those old pine trees

The distant sound of Him every night saying, "Come on back to Me"

The echoes in the mountains, crashing through the snow

Chasing you down that winding road no matter where you go


And although you may survive

Although you'll make it through

Move on with your life; there's nothing else you'd rather do


But deep inside, those echoes have become a part of you; you know they will never go, so here's what you can do


Just roll on with those echoes through those old pine trees

And run right to Him every night when He's saying, "Come on back to Me"

And roll right through those mountains and crash right through that snow

Sooner or later, you're gonna learn how to let go.


Can you hear the echoes?

# Chapter 1

## Phase One

I like to think of the first almost half of my adult life as my "phase one." And having said that, I want to start this book out right away with the fact that everything in life is temporary. Even life itself is temporary. So remember, no matter what phase you've had or which phase you are in right now, everything is temporary. So in my phase one, I had a knowledge of God, even a desire to lead others to Him, *but* a deep and intimate relationship and true understanding of my identity in Him, I did not have.

At this time in my life, I was working hard to build a health and fitness empire and reputation that would allow me to be admired and sought after by people. God had gifted me with a talent for coaching, teaching, and self-discipline, so I advanced in my job as a health coach and personal trainer. And I loved it. This somehow made me feel important. Validated. Loved.

Isn't it interesting that when most of us really meditate on why we do the things we do, it is because we want to feel loved and accepted by others? We all have our stories, our "whys" that have led us to certain points in our lives and into certain choices that we make. It was at my "phase one" phase in my life when I realized that it didn't matter how important I looked from the outside; on the inside of me, there was something significant that was missing.

Emptiness on the inside can often lead to messes on the outside. In my case, my messes looked like financial hardships, immoral relationships, deceitfulness, and zero long-term direction or plan.

I was a professional athlete, sought-out personal trainer, fitness model, published columnist, and radio show cohost. Many people had put me on a pedestal and looked to *me* for advice and support.

Even I had deceived myself into thinking I was happy and fulfilled. Despite the level of behind-the-scenes messes that were really going on, I did have a heart for the Lord. I hosted my own fitness expos where I gave speeches teaching people how to care for their bodies and their health, and with each slide I would show in my presentation, I would have a scripture attached to back it up. Those scriptures were provided by my mom, who would help me pick the best ones to use for what it was I was trying to teach.

I knew God was real. I knew in my heart that there was a good plan for me and for my life. The problem was I was too busy trying to make it all happen for myself and too busy *not* obeying Him. I was choosing to stand in the way of my destiny and choosing to do things my own way rather than God's way. Notice I said I was choosing. How many times in life do we want to blame God for the trials that come into our life, when what we really need to be doing is taking responsibility and realizing we were the ones who made the choices that put us in the circumstance to begin with, not God?

Of course, God loves you and me and will work all things for our good, but He will never interfere with our free will or choices. He may send people or circumstances to attempt to get us back on His path, but at the end of the day, it is up to us to build that relationship with Him, know His Word, obey His Word and make our own decisions. You will see that I focus heavily on the subject of choices throughout this book because it truly can be a make-or-break option for us in life.

And so, my "phase one" looked as though I was on top of a mountain until the day I was knocked all the way down into one of the deepest valleys of my life.

# Chapter 2

## Forever Changed

The stick was sitting on the bathroom counter. I had done this before; surely it would be fine. Sure, I was late, but that wasn't uncommon for me, especially due to the lean muscle mass and hefty workout load I carried. I honestly took the test thinking it would show the same exact ways it had shown in the past. Negative. I was so convinced that it was nothing that I took it, set it on the counter, and went about my day, forgetting it was even there.

Before running out of the apartment to meet clients, I ran in to use the restroom, and as I sat on the toilet, I picked up the forgotten stick just to be sure. Wait just a minute. Close your eyes. Open them back up. There are two lines there today instead of one.

My heart sank. No way! *That can't be right*, I thought to myself. In a sheer moment of panic, I texted and canceled my clients and took myself directly to the drug store up the street, where I purchased just about every type of pregnancy test that they had available.

A couple of hours later, as I sat on the floor in that third-story apartment, I was surrounded by numerous pregnancy tests. They all read "positive." It's hard to say exactly what I was feeling at that moment, excitement for the life that I was carrying inside of me, but mostly I felt fear.

You see, I knew I was a mess. I knew I was making irresponsible choices in my life. If I was such a disaster of a human being, how could I possibly take care of a baby? I was terrified.

What would everyone say? I felt such embarrassment. What would everyone think? I felt such shame.

I was pregnant at probably the most inopportune time, in what was probably one of the most inopportune ways.

A baby. I was going to be a mama.

Shortly after discovering the news, I started to get sick. And not just pregnancy sick. I noticed the lymph nodes in my armpits were quite swollen. My exhaustion was next level. I began to get rashes on my chest and stomach. My legs felt so incredibly heavy. Of course, most of the people who knew were telling me it was just the pregnancy, and it was to be expected. On the phone with my mom one day, I explained. As any mom would be, she was worried. I was missing a ton of work due to being sick. I hadn't told anyone at work that I was pregnant. I had a team of competitors whom I trained that were preparing for shows. I was exhausted, overwhelmed, and so scared! My mom and dad gave me the option to go stay with them. "Let's just get you through this pregnancy, and then you can regroup."

When all else fails, move back home, right? I was so ashamed and embarrassed that I didn't tell my clients the truth. I simply told them I was going for an extended visit and didn't know when I would be returning. (To date, I have never returned to Colorado.) I suddenly found myself in my early thirties with no job, no clients, no home of my own, no money, and living at home with my parents. Did I mention that I was a mess? If a situation could ever feel hopeless, mine sure did.

But there was one thing that we all had to look forward to. One thing that was more important than any of these other things.

There was a baby! I never knew for sure if I would become a

mom. I was 110 percent terrified. But my baby gave me hope. My baby gave me a reason to believe and to press on. God gave me my baby because God knew the choices that I would make because of my baby and the transformation that would soon come into my life. God knew that I needed my baby, and He had given him to me in His perfect timing and in His perfect way, not mine.

# Chapter 3

## Alex

The first moment you see and hold your child is something you never forget. Alex was born on April 9, 2013, via all-natural vaginal birth at forty-two weeks along. He was perfect. Despite the diagnosis during pregnancy of an autoimmune disease that most say should have terminated my pregnancy or even killed me, God had brought us through and entrusted a perfect, beautiful baby boy to me. I can't help but still cry just writing those words. You see, the biggest lesson I hope you get out of this book, the biggest aha moment I pray you receive is that *no matter what your circumstances may look like*, God can and will work it for your good if you love Him and seek Him. He will lift you out of the valleys and set you on the mountain tops if you will let Him and if you will choose Him over yourself.

Every time I looked at Alex, I felt complete despair over the choices that I had made that landed my child and me in this position. How could I be so irresponsible? But at the same time, every time I looked at Alex, I had a deep yearning and desire to do better. To be better. To give him a good life. I had never felt such an unconditional and sacrificial type of love before; sweet Alex had changed me forever.

I never had the "why me" mentality regarding the situation I was in, nor did I place blame elsewhere. I put myself in this position, and I put Alex in this position as well.

It was during this time that I remember feeling a fire inside of me that I had never felt before; it was a burning desire to change. To change my ways. To learn to do better.

My motivation was not myself; it was Alex. Alex deserved a good life. Alex deserved a healthy mom. My entire motivation wasn't even to please the Lord yet; it was entirely Alex.

Jesus was my Lord and Savior, and I found hope in Him, but Alex was saving me day by day by motivating me to radically seek the Lord and learn a new way of living with Him.

As unideal as this circumstance was, I now know that God was using it as a way to pursue me. He had always pursued me. He had always loved me and been with me, but I had never received any of that from Him, much less surrendered my life and chased after Him.

God knew that it would take having baby Alex in these unideal circumstances and for me to personally hit "rock bottom" for me to chase Him and His will for my life. God is good.

All of the time. Even when we are not. God will never leave us nor forsake us, even when we feel like He isn't there.

He is always there. If we choose and allow Him, He will always work on our behalf for good.

Do you know that He is always pursuing you also? And a lot of the times, in your hardest times, He is pursuing you the most, just hoping that you will finally give up on yourself and your ideas and your ways and trade them for His so that you can have all that He wants you to have. He pursues us through people, through circumstances, through pain, and through victory. You never have to look too far or listen too hard to see and hear Him if you truly try.

I want to pause for just a minute and ask if anyone reading this has ever made some choices that affected your children in a negative way. Whether it be relational, financial, or just a mistake you made.

News flash, we all make bad choices and mistakes that can affect our children badly, and most of the time, most of us don't intend to do that. As a result, we all can carry heavy loads of guilt and shame because we know better and because we want to do better for our kids. I often felt that way when I would look at Alex. I was going to do whatever I could to make his life good for him, but I still felt terrible for putting us in such a hard situation to begin with. The guilt was something I carried with me for a long time until one day, in my prayer time, the Lord put something on my heart about it; this is all a part of Alex's story. This is all a part of his journey. I cannot rob him of that or "protect" him from it because who am I to do that? We all have our own stories and testimonies that we can use to help people and to glorify God, and Alex's story is part of a bigger plan, God's plan for him.

Maybe you have a similar situation happening for you and your children or for someone you know. Maybe the choices you made put yourself and your baby or babies in unideal circumstances. Let me just ease your mind and your heart a bit here; those babies belong to God. God has a plan and purpose for them, just like He does for you, and you have an obligation to share their story with them because it is a part of their own journey and their own story that God will use.

Alex belongs to God, and God knows exactly what Alex needs and how to care for him now and for the rest of his life. I trust God with Alex, and I rest easy knowing I made the best decision I could make to love and protect my baby. I hope any parent who may read this can also believe this for their children.

# Chapter 4

## The Turning Point

Alex was such a happy baby. He was growing and healthy and brought me and my mom and dad such joy. During the first year of his life, my mom helped care for him so I could go out and find new clientele and start making a living again. It was not easy. We lived in a very small town in Kentucky where health and wellness didn't seem to be on the priority list for most, so I was driving myself an hour each way to a bigger town, Lexington, where I had found a small personal training studio and had begun rebuilding my clientele. Two days a week, I made the drive and was working hard to find new clients. I was not making much money at all, but at this point, anything helped. I was almost in my mid-thirties and hated being dependent on my parents to care for my child and me. While I was pregnant, the dynamic at my parents' house had been well. I mean, considering the circumstances I had put us all in, we had come together and made the best of it. They had been very supportive regardless of my irresponsible choices.

My upbringing was an interesting one. I don't feel like this book should go into a lot of those details, but I will say there was some instability and I had been through some abuse. I had chosen to move out of my parents' home at a pretty young age, and for most of my young adult life, I lived over one thousand miles away from them. Although we did talk via phone almost daily, and even though I would have said that we were close, I believe the physical distance was something that helped our relationship.

I believe my parents did the best they knew how to do. Again, we all have our stories and journeys, and I choose to be thankful for the good things and not dwell on—or be defined by—the bad. I also will never share or discuss anything with the intent to be dishonorable to my parents. I believe that my transformed life and the fruitfulness of my life and relationship with the Lord now honors them.

Throughout the course of my life, and throughout Alex's and my stay with my parents, there tended to be a lot of drama. (Outside of the drama that I had brought.) Instability is probably the best word I can use to describe it. Never knowing from day to day what things would be like or what you might say or do that could cause an uproar.

One day my mom and I were having a conversation in her living room. She was upset with my dad about something, and, looking back now, I'm sure the things that she told me may have been over-exaggerated since her emotions were running higher than normal. She had shared with me how she had to "force my dad to play with my brother and me" when we were younger. That he would come home from work, and had it not been for her, he wouldn't have had much at all to do with us. Of course, I don't believe this is true now, but at the time, I put a lot of merit in what she had to say, and I wondered if it was true, and if it was, it was definitely hurtful to know about.

I don't recall the exact timeline, but weeks later (it was actually approaching Alex's first birthday), my mom, dad, and I had sat down for a family meeting. I can't remember exactly why she had requested this, but nonetheless, there we were. She was proclaiming that my dad and I needed to work on our relationship and our closeness, and I brought up the conversation that she and I had weeks before because it had been weighing heavily on my heart. When I confronted my dad with the information that I was given, it looked as though I had just sucker-punched him in the gut. I remember so clearly; he looked at my mom, and it was obvious that he was hurt and that he felt betrayed. He didn't say much. He simply got up and walked out of the house. I knew that he had just been deeply hurt, and I also knew that what my mom had told me was not true. She had simply been lashing out at him through her anger and told me something that she should not have.

Tempers are something that run strong in our family, especially on my mom's side. It is definitely not something anyone would want to be on the receiving end of.

I left the room with Alex and took him back for a diaper change. Moments later, my mom was standing in the doorway of Alex's room. "You're not my friend." Her face was red, and her tone was low. I knew I was in for it.

I don't remember all the exact words she used, but something to the effect of how I had just betrayed her, how I had hurt my dad, how I was a terrible person. With each phrase, she stepped closer and closer to me. I had zero opportunity to reply, not that it would have done any good anyway. I had seen her this way before, many times. This level of anger isn't something I could combat. Alex was lying on his changing table, so I stepped away a bit toward the middle of the room. She had come closer and closer and eventually was so angry and so close to me that she made the decision to start hitting me. In my face. Repeatedly. She probably slapped me a handful of times while I ducked and covered. As I stood back up, she then asked me in an angry and hateful tone, "Do you want to hit me, Jenny?"

"No, Mom, I'm not going to hit you," I replied. As she turned and walked out, I heard my dad coming in through the front door. "Well, I hit her," my mom said. "Good," my dad replied.

# Chapter 5

## The Tipping Point

I need to be very clear here. Sharing these pieces of my story is for one purpose and one purpose only; to glorify God and to share how He can work in your life just the way He has and is working in mine. The story wouldn't have the same power without certain pieces given, but again it is not intended to dishonor anyone or to prove me to be a victim. I am victorious through Christ, who is my strength, and I will use my story and my life to glorify Him and to help others. I also hold no ill will toward my parents or their actions and choices. I believe God is working in the situation, and I rest in that.

Alex had just had his first birthday prior to this occurrence. The thought of him growing up in and around the same instability that I had grown up in made me sick to my stomach. But what on earth could I do? I was in no position mentally or emotionally to care for him on my own, and I had zero financial ability to do so. I was living in complete hopelessness and despair. Crying out to God, asking Him to forgive me. Asking to help me change. Asking Him to lead me into a better life, into His promises for my son and for myself.

The following few days are a bit of a blur. It was stressful and uncertain, to say the least. I was trying to figure out what options I might have, which were zero, while I listened to my parents having conversations about how I needed to "get out" and how they were not going to bear my burdens any longer. If I could remember exactly how it came about, I would say, but

I don't. Somehow over the course of a few days, it was decided that Alex and I would leave. I remember it was not a pleasant decision or conversation, but it was evident I had worn out my welcome. Alex's first birthday had been the ninth. We had "celebrated" him that weekend, which I believe was the tenth or eleventh, and the incident had occurred on the eleventh or twelfth, I believe. It's so difficult to remember all the dates, but it's important to share because they are relevant to show the miracles that God had ahead for Alex and me. On that Monday, April 14, 2014, I packed my little white Audi sedan with about six trash bags in the trunk. I loaded up my son with zero clue where we would go or what we would do. I was terrified, but I also knew in my heart that, somehow, this would be best for Alex in the long run. I took a step in faith, believing that my Father would make a way where there was clearly no way to be seen.

Before we left, I sat Alex down and walked over to the couch to say goodbye to my mom. She was clearly in a state of some type of mental break. I had seen her this way before, but never quite to this extent. It's extremely heartbreaking to see someone you love struggle with something that can be so debilitating. She was sitting on the couch, rocking back and forth, repeating over and over, "God loves me, Jesus loves me, my husband loves me, I am valid, I am worthy." It was almost like she wasn't there. I put my arm around her and said, "Mom, I'm going to go." She jerked away from me. "Don't touch me," she replied.

I calmly got up and began to walk away. I then witnessed her throw herself onto the living room floor and then begin saying things like she didn't want to live. For God to take her. She was sobbing. Even now, it makes me cry remembering seeing her that way. Such a strong, beautiful soul but so tormented by something I can't understand. I called my dad as he was out working in his workshop. "Dad, you'd better come in; Mom's having an episode." He knew what I had meant. We had been through this before. As he came through the front door and walked past me, he said, "Thanks a lot, Jenny." The drama continued as my dad tried to get my mom into their room. It was one of the most heartbreaking and traumatizing moments of my entire life. The details of what happened next, I don't feel are necessary to write; I can say there was another blowup and more harsh words from my dad. As I held Alex and was backed up literally against the wall of their living room, I knew I just had to go! I had to go in that moment! And that is exactly what I did. With tears streaming down my face, I drove Alex and me to the end of that long gravel driveway. I looked left. I looked right. I pulled out and started our drive to Lexington with zero clue what we would do or where we would go.

But God!

# Chapter 6

## It's All about Choices

As I made the drive, I could feel the inside of my body breaking down. High blood pressure, inflammation, nausea, high levels of fear, and anxiety. I was still such a mess inside. I had spent the last almost two years (my pregnancy and Alex's first year of life) pursuing God's word. Reading, seeking, and listening to teachers and preachers daily. I was trying, but I was still so far from the transformation I so eagerly wanted.

I had not yet learned how to walk by faith alone. I still wanted everything to make sense. I still wanted to take care of myself. I still wanted to "prove" that I could do it. I needed a wealthy man. I needed a high-paying and important job. I needed to make my own way. I was still such a baby Christian, lacking in maturity. Because of these thoughts, these limiting beliefs and inaccurate belief systems, I was still stuck in vicious cycles of behavior even in these dire moments. I needed to allow God to break these chains off me once and for all. What was I missing?

Thank God that He doesn't care about our messiness; all He wants is our hearts and our love. Thank God He will never give up on us, no matter what!

I pulled into the parking lot of the training studio where I was working part-time. It was the only place I knew to go. I knew no one. I had no friends. I had no money. I thought maybe the owner of the studio would allow Alex and me to stay at the studio until I could figure something out. There were soft mats on the ground we could lay on and a bathroom with a shower.

I could make it work if she'd allow it.

I gathered up my son out of the car and wiped my tears. "I will not cry. I will be strong," I said to myself as I walked toward the door.

As soon as she saw me, Sue came running across the room. I had been so caught up in the day's events I hadn't even bothered to look in the mirror. "Oh my gosh, are you okay?" she exclaimed as she approached me. Clearly, it was evident that I was not okay. The tears came pouring out. I could hardly speak. It was like this huge release of pent-up emotion was just coming out all at once. She grabbed Alex from me and took me over to sit down. I told her what had happened. I told her I had no place to go, but I knew I couldn't go back to where I came from. "Let me make a call," Sue said to me.

Let me pause here for a moment and explain to you the importance of our choices. We all know that God is God and that He can do anything at any time. We know that God is omniscient, omnipotent, and omnipresent. We know that God is the Alpha and the Omega, the beginning and the end. He is God Almighty! So why do bad things happen? Why doesn't He just reach down and fix everything for us or give us some magical billboard to tell us exactly what to do and when to do it? God can do anything, but one thing God will not do is interfere with our ability to choose. In the beginning, God gave Adam and Eve the gift of free will. It is a gift we all still have today. God can and will work everything for good, but God will never interfere with our choices. This is something I've learned to love so much about God. That He will allow me the ability to decide my life. To choose my path. To choose Him. To choose to radically pursue His promises for me. How amazing! Back then, I didn't understand how to make choices that put God first; I only knew how to walk by what I could see, and then in the midst of the mess I would create, I would then ask God for His help.

Now I know how to live with such a reverential fear of doing *anything* that isn't God's will for my life despite what I want. Sure, I have desires in my heart, but my prayer is not for God to help me make all of them come true; my prayer is that He helps me sort through them, and those that are His will come to fruition, and the others do not. I only want God's will in my life, period.

**This leads me to the first life tip that I want to share with you: Be afraid of doing life and making decisions without God.**

I am not talking about fearing God in a way that He's going to be mad at you, or if you don't do the right thing, you've lost your salvation, or that He will be forever disappointed with you or won't love you anymore. This has already been fully taken care of in the finished works of Jesus on the cross. What I am talking about is a reverential fear of God. Being so dependent on Him to lead you and guide you into new plans, opportunities, adventures, and choices that you completely relinquish your will in exchange for His. Your top priority in your daily life is to ask Him for His wisdom, His favor, and His guidance. Your prayers are bold and strong, but you also come to Him humbly stating that you only want favor in the areas that are His will for your life. Be terrified to live life without God front and center, and let Him know that you are!

This is such an important part of living a truly transformed Christian life. If we are not living in the will of God for our lives, we will never be happy, no matter how much we have. It is only when we are truly living out the purpose that He has put on our lives that we find fulfillment, joy, and true transformation.

Be afraid to do life without God. Be afraid to get to the end of your life not fulfilling His will for you.

Decide today that you'll have this reverential fear that will lead you into the promises of God for your life.

When Sue came back into the room, she knelt by me and said, "It's going to be okay."

Isn't it amazing how kind people can be when they see someone in need? You may not know the people that God will put in your path when you need them the most. I sure didn't have any idea the ways that God would work, and if I had chosen to stay where it seemed "safe" (or safer than where I was), if I had chosen to not step out in faith even though I was terrified, I would have missed all the glory that God was about to give me. A lot of the times when God is orchestrating changes in our lives and in us, it is highly uncomfortable for us. This is one of the ways our faith grows. The conscious willingness to get uncomfortable and trust God despite what things look like pleases God and brings us closer to Him.

Sue told me that her mother, who was a widow, lived about ten minutes away and would be happy for Alex and me to come and stay with her while I figured things out.

Hallelujah! A warm bed, a roof over our heads, and a kind soul to fellowship with. I sure didn't see that coming, but God knew!

It was a quaint brick house with a good-sized yard. She had lived there for years. I was so incredibly thankful, and I made sure that she knew that. Alex and I slept in the back bedroom, and even though there was no bathtub for him, he fit comfortably in her kitchen sink. I was able to grab a few groceries for us, making sure Alex was my priority and getting all of his essentials. Every night I would turn on Alex's Jesus bear (a stuffed bear that had a recorded box inside of it that spoke scriptures, purchased for him by my mom, actually), and we would both fall asleep listening to the different verses about who we are, His love, and His promises for us. I knew this was a temporary situation. I was thankful.

About two weeks passed, and I was busy trying to find some new clients. I couldn't go get a "job" because that would require Alex going to day care, and I couldn't afford that, not to mention the thought of not being with him nearly killed me. I couldn't find a place to live until I made more money. The only solution I could come up with was to keep going around town searching for opportunities to build relationships so I could try to build my personal training clientele. This would take time. A lot of time.

Sue allowed Alex to come to the studio with me, and although I paid her a percentage of my earnings, if I could fill my client book, we would be okay. How was I going to find the people? Remember, I really didn't know anyone in this town. Not to mention, no one knew me. Back in Colorado, I had been a highly sought-after personal trainer. New clients were never an issue for me there. But here, I felt like I couldn't even give away my services to people. Each day I would show up at the studio hopeful someone would walk in looking for sessions, and I would be the one who signed them up. I sat and made phone calls to other local businesses asking if I could host events or do a pop-up table to offer my services. After almost three weeks of trying, nothing much was happening. And even worse, the money that I did have, which wasn't much, was dwindling fast. Between baby cereal, diapers, groceries, and gas, I wasn't sure if we would make it another week. Something needed to happen, and it needed to happen fast! Despite the way my circumstances looked, I made great efforts to trust God.

I stayed close to Him. I trusted that He would make a way, just like He had with Sue's mom.

I didn't know when, and I didn't know how, but I clung to Him.

I clung to Him because there was no one else to cling to. God let me hit rock bottom because He knew that would be the thing that would bring me closer to Him and eventually would lead me into personal transformation and into His will for my life. I didn't know, but He knew.

Aside from all these stressors that I was facing, I was also having to deal with my mom. In hindsight, it seems to me that she may have thought that I would be back with Alex. Perhaps she thought I would apologize and ask for forgiveness and beg to come back "home."

This obviously was not the case, and as a matter of fact, I had made up my mind that we would not go back to that situation, no matter what. She did not like it. She did not like it at all.

Each day my phone was flooded with messages and texts from her. Hateful, nasty, threatening messages. If she was trying to make me afraid, she was doing a good job. I wasn't afraid of her threats, but I was afraid of her. The instability and insanity of her messages were next-level.

She did scare me because I didn't know what she was capable of in this state of mind. Still, I somehow looked for the good. I somehow was heartbroken and in tears over her harsh words, accusations, and hate toward me. I still somehow wanted my mom's love and approval, and she still had me convinced that everything was my fault and that I was just a mess of a person who would never change.

The thing about my mom, I only know how to compare her to Jekyll and Hyde. One day she's loving, kind, and fun. But then... Right in that moment, I was living in the "but then..." that was a million times worse than I could have ever imagined. My mom thought I would need her and that I couldn't make it without her.

The one thing she forgot was that I am God's child, and He was all that I needed.

# Chapter 7

## Living within Miracles

It had been about three weeks since Alex and I had moved in with Sue's mom. Although she had not put a timeline on how long we could stay, I knew I needed to figure something out and wanted to do so sooner rather than later.

I'll never forget the day I received a message from one of my fellow trainers from the studio. Her name was Morgan, and we had struck up a bit of a friendship, being we were at the training studio each day together. I had shared pieces of my situation with Morgan, and we had collaborated on some ideas to infuse more clients into the studio for both of us. Again, God works through people, and sometimes they themselves don't even realize that.

"I have something I want to talk with you about. Can we meet for lunch?"

The message read something like this. Morgan was having a few issues at the studio with Sue (I believe it was some type of dispute over clients, as Sue also trained clients in the studio).

Morgan had shared with me some frustrations she was having, and I figured she just wanted to meet for lunch to vent or maybe get some advice or input.

I grabbed a high chair for Alex and sat down in the grocery store café. We exchanged a little bit of small talk before Morgan did something that literally would change the trajectory of my life forever.

"John's getting transferred to Georgia for work, and we are going to be moving. I want you to take my book of clientele. I feel like you're best equipped to offer them what they need." She pushed a huge stack of folders across the table toward me.

"Morgan, what?" "Shock" was not a big enough word. "I can't believe this. I don't know what to say."

"One more thing," she said, smiling. "We leave next week, Monday to be exact." (That day was Friday.)

"We have a three-bedroom, two-bathroom house in Nicholasville that will need some tending to while we get it ready to sell. If you'll take care of our two dogs, I'd love for you and Alex to stay there. Rent free, of course, in exchange for caring for it and the dogs."

> Even youths grow weary and tired, And vigorous young men stumble badly, But those who wait for the Lord [who expect, look for, and hope in Him] Will gain new strength and renew their power; They will lift up their wings [and rise up close to God] like eagles [rising toward the sun] They will run and not become weary, They will walk and not grow tired.
>
> Isaiah 40:30–31

Was this really happening? I was having to pinch myself and ask. The emotion that welled up in me is something I cannot put into words. Do you see how the walking-in-faith way always makes a way, even when we see no way, even when we are standing right on the ledge and need clients and money within a week to buy diapers and baby food? He always makes a way when we learn to trust and fully surrender to Him.

Easter was on April 20 that year. (If you recall, we had left my parents' house on April 14.) I wanted Alex to get to experience an Easter egg hunt. A quick Google search had landed us at a large local church in Lexington. I hadn't been to church in years. Growing up, my parents never really had found a "church home," and it had not been an important part of our lives. So naturally, into my adulthood, it had not been an important part of my life either. I do not believe you have to attend church to have a close and intimate relationship with the Lord, and I believe, as Christians, that church is not just a building where we gather once or twice a week. We are the church. God works through us and in us to make His proclamation to the world. We are His representatives. If you don't attend a physical church regularly, you don't need to feel condemned about that. Seek God's will in your life, and if He desires for you to be attending a physical church, He will lead you there.

At this time in my life, I needed a place to go. I needed a place to be loved and to learn, grow and fellowship. God knew that, and that's exactly why He led me to that Easter egg hunt that day. He also knew the decision I would make to come to the end of myself and how fiercely I would choose to seek Him.

The egg hunt was outside, and Alex had a great time. While watching him, a woman had approached me and invited me to stay for Easter service. I was reluctant, to say the least. Alex had never been anywhere without me besides with my parents, and if I attended service, I would have to leave him in the kid's room. I also felt so uncomfortable. What would people say? What would people think? I didn't even know anyone, but for whatever reason, I decided to try. I walked through the doors of the church. We stopped quickly to take a photo with the Easter Bunny. (I still have this photo hanging in my office.)

I look at it often and always think to myself, *No one would ever know what we were going through by looking at this picture.* We can so easily mask our pain by throwing on a cute outfit and a pretty smile.

It was so hard to leave Alex. He cried; I cried. "We will text you if he doesn't get better," the day care worker assured me.

I walked into the sanctuary and located a seat in the back so I could sit alone. Wouldn't you know that a man came and plopped down next to me, attempting to strike up a conversation? I clearly wasn't in the mood, and he must have picked up on it because he quickly relocated his seat. *What is wrong with men?* I remember thinking to myself.

As service began, I had no clue what was about to take place for me. We hadn't made it ten minutes into the worship, and I was sobbing uncontrollably. I have always been a strong woman. Resilient, most would say. But I was in so much pain. Still carrying the shame and embarrassment of my choices. Still carrying the rejection and hate from my parents. Still carrying all of the brokenness inside that I had never dealt with. When the altar call happened, I didn't even think twice. This was my day. They gave me a Bible and a small wooden cross that read, "It's not too late." This cross still sits on my office shelves to this day.

I had given my life to Christ before. Technically I was six years old the first time I was saved. But something was different that day. I felt a shift inside of me. I felt a true surrendering of all that I was.

I didn't care anymore about myself or my desires. I only wanted Him.

I decided to give my life to Christ on April 20, 2014, in a radical way, and my life has never been quite the same.

God may not magically show up in your life, but He will magically show up in your life!

What do I mean?

Faith. Faith is the belief in things you cannot see. Faith is the belief in things that don't make sense. Faith is the belief in things that some may say are crazy. Faith is trusting and relinquishing.

**The second life tip that I want to share with you: Surrender. Relinquish all that you are, all that you want, all that you think, say, and do to Him.**

It seems that a lot of Christians live in what I will call "the gray." You love the Lord, you believe, and you want to live in the victorious life that Jesus died for you to have. But you've never truly surrendered all of you to Him.

As we will get to a little later, I remember my therapist asking me, "Jenny, do you want to get better?"

So, I ask you the same thing, do you want to get better? Do you want to live better? Do you want to do better? Do you want to be better? Most people would answer these questions quickly with a yes, forgetting that as Christians, in order to do this, it means we have to sacrifice, be separated from the flesh, from our habits, from our human desires apart from God, from our tendencies that aren't from God, from our dysfunctions, our addictions, our comforts. (Just to name a few)

Scripture states we must "cut off the old to be renewed into the new." Sounds unpleasant, doesn't it?

In my case, I refused to choose to do this on my own, so God allowed me to put myself into a place where I had no other option.

*God is after us. He wants us to live the life Jesus died for, and, friends, He will continue to pursue you and chase you down until you have what He desires for you to have.*

You will have to decide to surrender all that you are to Him. Lay it all at the foot of the cross. Copartner with God. Allow

Him to work, allow Him to take your burdens. Allow His will to be done for you.

I want you to do something with me right now. I want you to think of something that is currently in your life that you know is not from God. This could be a bad habit, addiction, stronghold, unbelief, fear, anxiety, or unforgiveness. I want you to close your eyes and literally picture the cross right in front of you. Now take that thing, or things, whatever they are, and walk yourself right up to the foot of the cross and lay them down there. Picture it. Feel it. Soak it in. Jesus has taken it all for you because He loves you. Just the way you are. Now I want you to turn around, walk away and leave it there. Leave it at the foot of the cross. It is time, friends. It is time to surrender. It is time to let it go. It is time to step into the abundance, peace, joy, health, and prosperity that has already been given to you because of Him.

To accept and receive it, you must lay all that you are apart from God at the foot of the cross.

You must choose Him, and you must decide to live your life entirely by faith.

Real-deal Christianity is not for cowards or wimps. Real-deal Christianity means you know and believe the promises of God are for you, and you want them, and you have the desire.

But in order to get from where you are right now over to that dreamy, purposeful place, there's typically a whole lot of work and change that must happen.

Unfortunately, I think many people, even Christians, are not up for that challenge, and that is why they fail to see the victory in their lives that they wish they could see.

Are you up for that challenge?

# Chapter 8

## The New Place

To this day, I don't know if Morgan was a believer. What I do know without a doubt is that God used her in my life. Miracles were happening right before my eyes; there was no denying that.

As I stated earlier, Morgan and Sue had been having some differences, and after Morgan's and my lunch that day, she had filled me in a little more. Her fiancé, John, had gotten the news months back actually that he could be transferred to Georgia; they just weren't sure exactly when it would happen. This was before I had come on the scene at the studio, and at that time, Morgan had mentioned to Sue that she would leave her clientele to Sue when the transfer happened.

Morgan was younger than I was, and we had a lot of the same training philosophies and used a lot of the same tactics with our clients. Sue, bless her, was a bit older and did cater to an older demographic of clientele. Now that I had come into the studio and Morgan had gotten to know me, she decided that she felt I would be better suited to train her clients versus Sue training her clients. Yikes! Of course, I was just becoming privy to all these details, and yes, it made me very uncomfortable.

Morgan had let Sue know her decision, and her clients were now caught in the crossfire. And then there was me. I can only imagine what Sue had thought. She had helped me so much, and here I was, taking Morgan's clientele. It got real ugly real fast. As quickly as God had moved and made miracles, the enemy came against me again through circumstances that had been out of my control. Sue was angry and offended. Her mom was angry with me as well and acted in disgust toward me as I packed the car to head to Morgan's house that next week. I had told Morgan that I wanted to do the right thing. I had appreciated so much that she would leave her book of clients to me, but I did not want to upset Sue.

So, we decided the fair thing to do would be to let the clients decide for themselves who they wanted to continue their training with.

Morgan made the calls and sent the messages in a professional and caring way to let her clients know she would be leaving, and they could either continue their training with Sue or me.

Some choose me, and some choose Sue. I then received a message from Sue that I was no longer welcome to train in her facility. Clearly, she blamed me for the "loss" of these potential clients for her.

Great! Now what?

Sue was so angry with me. She was so hurt and so offended, and to this day, I never got to have a conversation with her. For months and even years to come, she would try to sabotage me and my ability to work in the city of Lexington. The same woman who had helped me and been so kind was now the woman who was trying to destroy my ability to work.

Morgan was headed out of town, and I had let her know I needed to find a new place to train her clients.

"I'm going to introduce you to some old friends. They own a studio on the other side of town; maybe you can work something out with them."

The husband-and-wife couple was about my age, and they

seemed like great people. We met at the studio initially because it was under construction, and they wanted to show me what they had going on. It was really going to be a beautiful facility. I had owned a studio and a gym of my own in the past, so I could appreciate all that they were doing with this facility. The initial meeting went well, and it quickly led to another sit-down meeting. We all sat at the table. They knew Sue and had briefly asked what had happened. I was honest and told them how bad I felt that things had happened the way that they had. I could tell they were honest people and loyal people. They were kind, but it was also clear they were serious about business. He looked at me and asked, "Do you have an accredited certification?"

"Yes," I lied. I had been certified for years and years as a trainer. I had taken numerous continuing ed courses, even nutrition courses, but sometime during my pregnancy with Alex, my certification had lapsed. I had been so consumed with everything happening in my life that I failed to do the continuing ed credits to keep my certifications up to date. Even though I was able to still carry liability insurance, my certification credentials had officially expired.

I couldn't possibly tell him the truth. That would mean that I would have no place to train these new clients, and it would also mean I would have no income. Alex and I were out of money, and I was desperate. It would come back to bite me later, but for now, I had found a place to train and make money. And despite another bad choice, a lie, God would still love me and work it out for my good.

My plan was to try to save the $1,200 it would take to retest and acquire a valid certification again.

I just needed to buy some time.

Not only did I start at the new studio training my new clients, but they also offered me the opportunity to teach their 5 a.m. classes. It was early, but the pay was good, and I knew I could build more relationships that would eventually add more personal training clients. On top of allowing me into their studio, they opened their home to Alex. They wouldn't allow me to bring him to the studio with me, and they had a nanny who cared for their young son at their home. I can't remember exactly what I paid, but I remember it was reasonable, and I was thankful that Alex was in a beautiful and safe home while I was working to provide for us. Again, I knew it was a short-term solution, but I was so thankful.

Alex was doing well, and that was all I cared about. He was happy and safe.

He had taken his first steps in the living room at Morgan's house, and despite the complete chaos and uncertainty in our lives, he had a way of filling me with sheer joy. I desired so much for Alex to have a stable and loving home, and I was willing to do whatever God asked me to do to provide that. I still had a long way to go in my walk with Him, but I could feel myself changing little by little, day by day.

In the meantime, the harassment from my mom had continued. She had a way of tearing me apart one day and then reeling me back in the next. During my stay at Morgan's, my mom had texted me some of the worst messages I've ever received in my life. Accusing me of awful things and even threatening to try to take Alex from me. The stress was too much to carry. My body had broken out in shingles, and I had lost a significant amount of weight. I was so exhausted, but I knew I could not give up. I had to keep moving forward. I had to continue believing and trusting God. He had brought me that far; I knew He would not fail Alex or me. I just had to keep going.

As chance would have it, there was another trainer who worked at this new studio, and it turns out he was Sue's personal trainer. (Yes, even trainers hire trainers sometimes.) I had a bad feeling. He was never friendly and pretty much avoided me like the plague. I just had to stay focused. Go to work, do my job to the best of my ability, come home, take care of my son, repeat.

I wasn't there to make friends; I was there to make a living for myself and my son. I was doing that, and it was going well. Since I had a free place to stay, I was able to save some cash pretty quickly. I had been in close contact with Morgan, and I knew it was only a matter of time before they would need to get her house on the market, which meant that Alex and I would need to make another move, and this time, I hoped it would be into our own place. I would need a deposit and the first month's rent, and I longed for a nice and safe place for Alex.

One day, out of the blue, I received an unexpected letter in the mail. It was from the IRS, of all things. Over three thousand dollars for an overpayment of past taxes is what the letter stated. What are the odds?

This would be enough to get Alex and me into our own place. I was elated. Thank You, Lord, thank You! I remember driving up Winthrop Drive one afternoon between clients. I saw a beautiful apartment complex that was just being completed. Could I afford that? Ideal location, safe, new. There were pools, putting greens, and even a huge pond in the back filled with ducks and geese. Alex and I walked into the office and asked for a tour. The apartments were beautiful, and because I had received this unexpected gift from God in the mail (IRS check), I was able to secure a second-floor, two-bedroom, two-bathroom apartment with a garage that overlooked the pond, had an amazing balcony, and beautiful sunset views. "When can we move in?" I asked. The woman handed me the keys. "Whenever you would like."

I made the drive back to Morgan's house, letting her know I had found a home for Alex and me and we would be sleeping there that night. She had recently picked up her dogs, and they were preparing to list their house any day now. The irony of how the timing was all working out.

Alex and I had no furniture with us yet, not because I didn't own any furniture, but because it was being stored in an old farmhouse on my parents' farm. I obviously had no clue how I was going to navigate that issue since my mom was being ruthless as of late in all her messages to me. I borrowed some blankets from Morgan's house and made up a place for Alex and me to sleep on my bedroom floor.

I loved this apartment so much. One thing I've learned in life is that when I chase God first, the blessings come, and the blessings seem to be so much more meaningful than they would have been if I had been chasing them first rather than chasing God. I knew God had given us this home. It was perfect; I was so thankful.

# Chapter 9

## Bonnie

I had interviewed a handful of girls from a reputable nanny website. The couple I worked for had been clear that they'd be happy for Alex to stay with their in-home nanny for a while, but I would need to figure something out soon. Most days, I was at the studio by 5 a.m., so finding someone who was able to watch Alex that early was not an easy task. I hired a few different young girls so that I could rotate the schedule and have backup if needed. The apartment was looking beautiful, and after I had let my parents know that I had found a place and I would need to have movers come to retrieve my items, it seemed that my mom had a bit of a heart shift. Maybe it was because she realized that her threats and tactics weren't going to work. I was not coming back home. Maybe because she realized that she wanted to see Alex, and as things were before, that was not going to happen. In hindsight, most would probably say I was crazy to allow her back "in" our lives, especially after the things she had accused me of and all of the things she had said to me. This had been one of the patterns of our family's life. Having a knock-down, drag-out blowup that most would never recover from, and then without resolve, move on as if nothing had happened. Such a mess. By the holiday season, my parents had been to visit my apartment a few times. My dad had even helped me hang curtains. My mom would meet me halfway once or twice a week to pick Alex up for the day so they could spend time with him. This was something they enjoyed, and at the time, it was helpful for me so I could save some money not having to pay for sitters or nannies. I was working a lot of hours, but with the percentage I had to pay the training studio, I wasn't living in an overabundance of cash. Alex and I still attended the church that we had been to on Easter, and I had joined a Life Group there and attended a recovery service every Thursday night called The Mat. I knew I still needed a lot of transformation in my life, and although there were some things I was willing to surrender to God, there were still some things I was still holding onto.

*"Jenny, do you want to get better?"* Bonnie asked me. I'm certain my face had a look of bewilderment on it. *"Of course I want to get better; why else would I be here?"*

I met with Bonnie once a week in her home office. She had been referred to me by a client of mine, and although I had been to therapy before, there was something about my experience with Bonnie that was different. She was in her sixties and well-rooted in her relationship with the Lord. I knew that the things she was telling me weren't just her opinions, they were things that were backed by scripture, and that is exactly why this experience had been so different and impactful for me.

I had made the initial call to set up an appointment because, despite my efforts in church, Life Group, and daily time with God, there were still areas of my life that I was struggling with, and I knew I needed to change them. I also knew this would be another expense for me, but it was necessary to break these chains off of me, not only for myself but for Alex. I also knew that God would make a way as He always had. Bonnie had tried to schedule me for an initial hour session, as most therapists do. "I would like to book out a few hours if that's possible," I had said. No way would an hour be enough time to make any progress. I wasn't going for fun; I was going for transformation, and I was prepared to be as radical with that as I could. I was nervous. I had my notebook in hand and my phone in case my mom called needing something for Alex.

This was my moment. My moment to be honest. Sure, I would have to take the blame for the messes I had created in my life, but it was worth it to me if I could change and do better for Alex.

Bonnie sat and listened and took notes for about two hours while I spilled out my life story. The good, the bad, the ugly, and everything in between. I didn't hold anything back. I was not there to play the victim. I was not there to place blame or make anyone look bad. I was there for one reason and one reason only.

To take responsibility for my life and to learn how to do things differently. It may sound crazy, but I really did not know how to do things differently than what I had always done.

"I guess that's about it," I said to Bonnie. I was trembling. I had been crying on and off, I didn't know what she was going to say, but I was prepared for the worst. I had just told her what a despicable human being I had been. How selfish and disgusting I had been. Would she even be able to help a person like me? I wondered. That's when Bonnie said something that I will never forget for as long as I live. She had laid her pencil down on the pages of notes that she had just taken and looked me straight in the eye.

"Jenny, statistically speaking, you should be a drug addict, an alcoholic, a stripper, or a prostitute. Being that you are none of those things, and being that you're sitting in this chair right now saying what you're saying and doing what you're doing, is amazing. I want you to know that you are amazing."

Was she serious? How could this be true? Nonetheless, her words pierced deep into my soul, and I suddenly didn't feel so dirty anymore. I had walked around for so many years feeling such heavy levels of dirt, shame, and disgust in myself.

Lord knows I had not done things the right way over the years, but somehow, I felt confident that I could change and that I could forgive others and forgive myself.

I found comfort and healing in that, and you should do so too. Even if I had been any of those things that Bonnie listed, it wouldn't have mattered. Jesus came for all of us! All! The many stories in the Bible show us that the worst of the worst were redeemed and transformed through Jesus. Murderers, adulterers, prostitutes. Jesus came for everyone and is no respecter of persons.

Come to Him and do your part and watch what happens in your life!

**The third life tip that I want to share with you: Take radical responsibility for your life. You are not a victim. It may not be your fault what has happened to you, but it is your fault if you don't take responsibility for where you are right now and copartner with God to step into His promises for your life. This is where radical change and transformation begin.**

I continued to meet with Bonnie as I was able. Each time we met, she would teach me something new about who I was, how I could change, and how good I was. She even told me that I was an amazing mother. She would help me dig into scripture and discover new truths and leave me with homework to do until the next time we would see one another.

Bonnie played an essential part in my healing, but in order to receive what she gave me, I had to be willing to step out in faith yet again, relinquish my pride and ego, be honest and be willing to take responsibility and also receive grace. Grace is not just a word; it is a person, and His name is Jesus. God Himself humbled Himself and came in the form of a human man to fulfill the law and allow us eternal life with Him in heaven, but also abundant life here on earth. When you've accepted Jesus as your Lord and Savior and asked Him into your heart, you not only receive salvation with Him forever in heaven, but you also receive all that He fulfilled and did for you at the cross. Through Him, you have health, prosperity, abundance, protection, blessings, joy, peace, and fulfillment.

God can fix and do anything, but we have a part to play. Are you willing to do what God asks of you?

# Chapter 10

## My Prince in the Fireman Uniform

I was clearly in no shape to be embarking into a romantic relationship with anyone. But there was this guy. One of the many things I knew I needed to transform in my life was my relationships with men. Bonnie and I discussed this often. My views and thoughts about relationships and men were quite skewed, to say the least. I had grown up with an overbearing mother who, in my eyes, had "ruled the roost" and was disrespectful to my father, and my father, although he was a hard worker and provided for us, was rarely around, rarely involved, and didn't really lead our family as far as I could see. He also never pursued having a close relationship with me. It always felt extremely uncomfortable. This had led me into an early life seeking approval from boys, young men, and men. I would do just about anything for them to love and accept me, and at that time, I didn't have any clue about how sacred my body was and how I should protect and save it. This behavior had, of course, led me to deep-rooted feelings of shame and regret, even though I was too prideful to admit it back then. To top it off, some of the relationships ended up with major deceit and betrayal on their end, which caused my trust issues with men to only become worse. Knowing how to receive love from people has never been easy for me. It is something that I really have to intentionally work at.

Everyone who ever loved me or was supposed to love me typically hurt me, betrayed me, or mistreated me. So, love was not something I ever really understood.

Of course, I needed to take responsibility for where I was then, which was why I was seeking help to learn the correct ways that relationships should go according to God's Word.

I want to be very clear here; transformation doesn't happen overnight. A lot of the deep-rooted issues and pains that we carry are just that, deep-rooted. As we grow with God and learn how to discern Holy Spirit conviction (not condemnation) and character, we are continually renewed and transformed. This will be something that we work on and go through our entire lives. I love what one of my favorite sisters in Christ, and teachers of God's Word, says: "You may not be where you want to be, but thank God you aren't where you used to be."

As you are changing and growing in and with God, remember to focus on the progress you are making.

I love to keep journals. As I go back and read them, it reminds me how far I've come and when you see that proof of God working, it helps your hope grow stronger.

So, as I was saying, there was this guy. He had stopped in at Sue's studio one afternoon while I was working with a client. "I'm looking for Jenny" was what he had said. I thought maybe he was someone's husband stopping by to purchase some sessions maybe. I mean, how else would he know who I was?

"I'm Jenny," I had said as I walked over.

He was handsome. Charming. Dressed in his firefighter blues as he had just gotten off work.

"Hey, I'm Shane," he said as if I should know who he was. I'm sure a confused look was written all over my face as I searched my brain, trying to remember where I might know him from. "Rachel's friend. She told me you worked here, so I thought I would just stop by and say hello."

Rachel was a young client of mine. She had mentioned to me in one of our sessions together how they had a family friend who worked in the fire department with her dad and how she thought the two of us should meet. "He's so nice, and he's single," she had said to me.

"Girl, no!" I had replied to her. A relationship was the farthest thing from my mind. I was not interested.

Despite my adamant reluctancy, Rachel had still told Shane where the studio was and that he should stop in sometime and "just say hi."

"Well, I just wanted to come by and introduce myself. So, I'll let you get back to it. I hope you have a good rest of your day." And that was that. He just left. *Odd*, I remember thinking to myself. He didn't even ask for my phone number or anything. I went about my day not really thinking any more about it.

I did, however, send a text to Rachel stating how I had told her "no" and how she hadn't listened to me.

"Haha, I told you he was cute and nice." That was basically the only response I had gotten back from her; she obviously didn't feel bad about it.

About three weeks went by, and Shane stopped by again. This time I had Alex with me. Ironically enough, I was working with the same client I had been working with the first time he had stopped by. This time I greeted him with Alex on my hip. "Well, who is this little guy?" he asked. "This is Alex," I replied.

Alex was my top priority. Period. I knew that my old patterns with men could not repeat as they would affect Alex and his life in a negative way. Jesus was working in me, but I see so clearly how He was using Alex to "protect" me from myself. Areas in which I would have fallen back into old patterns simply were not an option anymore because I would not put Alex in those situations. Becoming a mom forced me to learn new habits and new ways of living. Becoming a mom forced me to run to God. Becoming a mom forced me into a new level of responsibility. I had not been willing to change for myself because I hadn't loved myself enough to do that. But Alex, I loved him enough to do it.

On this visit, Shane and I exchanged small talk, and this time he handed me a small card. "I know you're a single mom, and I thought you might enjoy this." A simple gesture of a gift card to an expensive and great restaurant in town. I was thankful. I was also still surprised that he left without asking for a phone number.

A few weeks passed, and I couldn't seem to get Shane out of my head. There was something about him that seemed different, a kindness. I broke and asked Rachel for his phone number, which of course, she was happy to give.

"Hey Shane, it's Jenny. I just wanted to reach out and tell you thanks again for the gift card. I took an older lady out with Alex and me, and we had a nice time."

We exchanged texts throughout the week and had our first official date a few weeks later.

We met at a local hibachi grill, where I talked his ear off for about two hours, devoured my food, and then asked him if I could finish what was left on his plate. Our relationship would continue to flourish, and God would continue to work in both of our lives for years to come.

One thing was for certain, Shane and I were both extremely broken people with broken pasts and deep-rooted issues. We also would learn that we are 110 percent the complete opposite in almost all things we do in day-to-day life. We would eventually see that despite our differences or how messed up we were, it would be our personal commitments to God and personal surrender of ourselves that would lead to a strong and blessed marriage and a life filled with God's love, grace, blessings, and mercies.

# Chapter 11

## Shane

Shane had been in his fair share of dysfunctional relationships, just as I had. He was almost forty years old and had never been married nor had children, although he had shared that all he ever really wanted was to have his own wife and family. Shane was raised Catholic, although he had also shared with me that as soon as he was old enough, he made the personal choice to leave that faith because there was a lot that didn't make sense to him personally. Although, at that time, he didn't have a full understanding of Christ and exactly what that meant for him, he did have a heart and love for God, and it would be our coming together in a dating relationship that would introduce him to teachers and preachers where he would become enlightened to the full truth of Christ and where his heart and life would also be transformed.

I have watched the Lord transform my husband over many years, and it has truly been amazing to witness. I am so incredibly proud of my husband for his commitment and willingness to grow in his faith and become a mighty warrior for the kingdom of God. My husband is truly one of the most self-sacrificial humans I've ever known. He is loyal, hardworking, and devoted, and he loves the Lord with all his heart.

We may get on each other's nerves in day-to-day life because we truly do everything the complete opposite way; it is true! But I wouldn't trade our life and marriage for anything, and I know that God brought us together and has truly blessed our life and our family. Shane is a blessing, and if you have the pleasure to meet him or call him a friend, you are certain to be blessed by that.

Shane had walked into my life at probably the most inopportune time. Can you imagine starting to date someone who was a recent homeless single mom with her life basically in shambles? Shane did not care about any of that. He saw my heart; he saw Alex. He loved Alex. Ironically enough, Shane's biological dad wasn't involved in his life at all, either. How wonderful that God would place a dad and earthly father into Alex's life that could relate personally to how he might feel.

Shane and I dated for a solid two years before he proposed to me, hanging a ring on a Wonder Woman Christmas ornament.

He and Alex had developed a strong bond, and I am forever grateful for his ability to love Alex unconditionally without any hesitation. Shane had met my parents, although he didn't speak much about it. The night he proposed, though, things changed. I had called my parents to share the celebratory moment, and rather than celebrating and congratulating, my mom did what my mom does; she made it all about her and completely ruined the entire night. I got off the phone in tears, and in that moment, Shane was very clear that he would support any decision I made to interact with my parents but that all he saw was a dysfunctional and toxic situation that he would not be a part of.

I'll never quite understand why my mom could never be happy for me throughout my life. I remember being published on the cover of a local health and wellness magazine, and rather than congratulations, she got mad because I hadn't mentioned her in the article. I could go on and on, but the point is I had some very big decisions to make for my life and for my family's life and how that would look with my parents.

I don't know if anyone reading this book has had to draw hard boundaries with family members, but here's what I want to say to you if you have; it is okay to protect your peace. It is okay to protect your joy. You are not responsible for other people's choices, actions, reactions, or feelings. You are only responsible for your own. Pray. Pray for your heart and pray for theirs, knowing that God is the only one who can truly change anyone. Read that again...*Stop* trying to change people. That is not your job. Love them, even if it's with distance. Pray for them, even if it feels unproductive. Lastly, believe that God is always working, and no matter what the outcome is, if you have controlled yourself and done your personal best to make godly decisions, you can go on with your life and live it to the fullest until it overflows with all that God has for you. You don't need to carry guilt, condemnation, shame, embarrassment, or responsibility for what you cannot control. Leave it at the cross and cling to all that you do have rather than putting your focus on what you don't have.

# Chapter 12

## "Keep Going, Jenny"

I'll begin this chapter with life tip number four: Staying stuck in your grief, your mindset, your limiting beliefs, your insecurities, or your pain is a choice you are making.

I imagine if I was on a stage in front of you right now, there may be some throwing tomatoes at me and booing me off the stage. But, friends, listen to me because I have lived this, and I understand. Jesus did not only come for you to have your salvation, but He also died so you could have all that He is. That means you have His confidence, His self-control, His peace, His joy, His wisdom, His prosperity, and His health, just to name a few, living inside of you.

Also, let me clarify, while it is important that we grieve and that we allow ourselves to walk with the Lord through our journey of healing and our own personal process, we must also have a level of awareness and be cautious that grief and pain aren't permitted to totally derail our life, prevent us from moving forward, or that we aren't continuously going around the same mountains repeatedly. If you find yourself feeling stuck, or repeating patterns, ask God to show you what you can decide to do differently to help you overcome and keep moving forward into His plan.

And then be ready. When He closes doors or opens doors, you'd better be willing and ready to roll up your sleeves and get to work.

We do not always choose the circumstances that come against us, and then there are times our choices do lead us into those circumstances, and then there are times the challenges come against us due to other people's choices. Regardless of how we come into trials, we do have the ability to decide to not sit in them and allow them to take over our lives that Jesus died for us to enjoy. We can decide how we react, how we feel, what we do, and what we don't do.

A lot of times, doing what is needed for us to heal, move on, or make necessary changes that, in fact, will bring us closer to God are not easy things to do. A lot of the time, they are choices that will bring us to our knees in complete despair and heartache. Learning how to forgive, let go of anger, not be bitter, and not harbor resentment are nearly impossible without God's help. Accepting that radical responsibility for your life and relinquishing it entirely to Him is not an easy task, despite what you might think.

Change is hard. Our flesh hates discomfort, and truth be told, our brains and bodies are hard-wired to keep us "safe and comfortable," so we are literally fighting an uphill battle when we choose change. You must stay strong in faith and cling tightly to Him to overcome the flesh and the temptations and desires to go backward once again into your "comfort" zone.

I always teach my kids this simple fact about life, "sometimes you may have to leave something behind in order to move into something greater that lies ahead."

This leaving behind can be actual physical things, but sometimes it may be things you can't physically see. Things like thoughts, feelings, habits, and beliefs.

Let's walk through a few examples together:

Perhaps you really need to work on your health. Maybe you have a good twenty pounds you should lose, but in order to do so, you're going to have to be willing to leave some things behind. You may have to give up soda or that sugar-filled pot of coffee every day in exchange for water; you may have to eat two cookies a week instead of two boxes; you may have to go out for a walk in the evenings rather than sitting in front of the TV. Your "comfort zone" will be to keep doing the same things that you're doing now, but in order to step into better health and a better version of yourself, you will have to be willing to leave those things behind. It is a choice, and your brain, and even your body, will tell you all the reasons why you can't or shouldn't get uncomfortable and change.

Another example might be; maybe God is trying to promote you to a nicer home or a better job. But in order for you to step into that, you must be willing to leave what you have now behind you. And even more challenging, He may ask you to leave it behind without knowing exactly what lies ahead. The majority of people will stay stuck where they are because they are too afraid of the unknown to step out in faith. They are still trying to control their lives and only step out when they can "see" the next steps. A lot of people also cling to the "old" and never make it into their promotions because their emotions are too tied to what they will have to leave behind, or maybe because what it's going to take to move out of where they are is going to be so difficult to do that they simply don't feel up to the challenge. Again, our strength, courage, and wisdom should not come from ourselves; we receive all of this in the finished works of Jesus. God never said our plan would be easy. He wants us to fully trust in Him, even when we do not understand and cannot see. If He has asked you to do something, He will get you through it, and you will be closer to Him because of it and a stronger person for it.

Let me be clear; I'm not telling you to be irresponsible. What I'm saying is if you truly feel God leading you away from something, you must take the steps even when you're scared, even if it's painful, even if it doesn't make logical sense. If you know it's what God is asking of you, you must step out in faith and trust Him.

"Jenny, how do I really know if God is telling me to do something?" This is a question we all ask. This is why having a close and intimate relationship with God is imperative. No other person can tell you with one hundred percent certainty what God's plan is for you, what the purpose is that He gave you, or what you should or shouldn't do. You must work with God to discover this for yourself.

Be brave. Be bold. Have faith. Believe that no matter what something looks like, He has a plan, and He will work all things for good because you love Him and you're called according to His purpose.

"And we know [with great confidence] that God [who is deeply concerned about us] causes all things to work together [as a plan] for good for those who love God, to those who are called according to His plan and purpose" (Romans 8:28).

One more example that I think is hard for most people; maybe you have a habit or an addiction that you'd like to get rid of, but you're not really willing to let it go. Remember the chapter about Bonnie; she asked me, "Jenny, do you want to get better?"

All of us would say "yes," that we want to get better. That we want to fulfill our purpose. That we want to do better and be better.

You do realize that you have to make the choice to leave the bad habits and addictions behind in order to get better, right? Are you really willing to do that?

Or are those habits and addictions too comfortable for you to let them go? Is the thought of not having or doing them just too scary? God cannot break those strongholds and chains off you until you truly and wholeheartedly are willing and make the choice to "get better."

Don't just say the words; mean it in your heart. And if you're struggling to do that, then pray that God will help you release the desire and change your heart so that you will be ready and willing to lay it down and truly let it go. This is when God can work.

Most times, habits and addictions begin because we are trying to escape pain of some kind or because we made a temporary bad choice not thinking much about it.

But habits and addictions stick around because they become comfortable for us, and we almost become dependent on them for the relief or feelings that they bring.

**Life tip number five: You can't get better until you're willing to let go and lean on God for relief rather than on habits and addictions.**

When I was nine years old, I developed an anxiety disorder. It began as a way for me to relieve my pain and stress, but into my adult years, it developed into a habit that I wasn't willing to let go of. It may seem easy enough to let go of things that are bad for us, but the comfort and ability to control something, especially when we feel like our lives are out of control, can be a stronghold that is very challenging to let go of. This has been a continuous struggle for me throughout my life, and I have to be constantly renewed in the Word of God and purposefully rely and depend on Him to comfort me in times of stress rather than choose to run to my bad habit.

Sadly, most people find it easier to stay stuck rather than face the truth or face the choices that will need to be made to move forward. Often fear, doubt, worry, or sheer pain keeps us from doing what God wants us to do. This is why Scripture so clearly teaches us to come to Him.

He knows that apart from Him, we cannot do what is necessary to fulfill His plans for us. He also knows we will never feel completely fulfilled in this life until we are living in the plan that He created for our life.

How many people go through their entire life never feeling completely fulfilled and never quite surrender all of themselves in order to step into their true purpose? Sadly, I think it's many.

Scripture tells us that as we grow in our relationship with the Lord, there will be a crucifixion of the flesh.

"And those who belong to Christ Jesus have crucified the sinful nature together with its passions and appetites" (Galatians 5:24).

I don't know about you, but I don't think that sounds extremely pleasant. I hate to be the bearer of bad news, but if you truly want to fulfill God's plan for your life and live in all that He has for you, you must be willing to accept some discomfort.

This is the predicament I found myself in with my parents. I could choose to stay stuck in the same vicious cycles that had plagued our family for years, or I could make a difficult and painful decision to break the cycle and step away from the dysfunction.

I love my parents. I miss parts of them. And I cherish the good memories we had over the years.

Not a day goes by that I don't think of them, and many times I wish I could pick up the phone and call just to hear their voice. I also know and have accepted the things that I cannot change and that the situation as it is will not be a healthy one for myself or my family to be in.

Making the decision to walk away from my family was so incredibly painful, and most days, I questioned if I was doing the right thing. I remember one day loading Alex into his stroller to go for a walk in the park. This was something we did often. Shillito Park was right up the street from us; it was beautiful, and I found such peace and time with God making the three-mile loop surrounded by nature and God's beauty.

This particular day I was really struggling. I was feeling all of the fear, doubt, pain, and questioning all of the decisions that I had made for Alex and me. At this time, we were living in the beautiful apartment that God had provided for us, and I was working my tail off training the clients that God had provided for me. Yet I was still struggling and questioning. I felt lonely, uncertain, and scared of what the future would hold for us. (The tearing away of the flesh and trusting in things we cannot see.)

As we started our walk that day, I was sobbing and crying out to God. I remember these exact words coming out of my mouth that day, "God, I need a billboard; please just give me a billboard and tell me that I'm doing the right thing." The walking path was a nice asphalt path that winded through the enormous trees and past beautiful creeks. We approached the halfway mark of our walk that day, and as I pushed the stroller around a corner and up a hill, I noticed something on the trail.

There was a Christian school nearby, and often times the kids would draw on the asphalt trail or leave scripture or messages for passersby to see. As I approached the words that were largely written in chalk, I expected to see an encouraging scripture or something fun that would make me smile. I was not prepared for what I saw: **"Keep Going, Jenny."**

The large words stopped me in my tracks. My name. At the exact time I was feeling so discouraged, doubtful, and scared. The exact time I was crying out to God for a "billboard."

I sat on the trail with Alex for a while, crying and praying. I also snapped a photo so I could always remember the day that God gave me my billboard and the courage I needed to keep moving forward.

God may not show up all of the time in my life that very way, but I will tell you, He always shows up! And He will show up for you too!

It's been many years since I've seen or spoken to my earthly parents. Mother's Day seems to be the most difficult for me, mourning the way I wish things were and remembering that they are not. I make a conscious choice to not allow myself to stay within those feelings. To not let it control my life or who I am. I also focus on all the good I do have in my life; rather than focusing on loss, I choose to focus on the good times we did have and all of the wonderful times I have now and will have in the future with my own family.

Life will always bring some levels of pain, heartache, loss, and discomfort. We all can choose to sit in the hate, the pain, and the anger. And if we decide to do that, then we decide to stay stuck.

So, although the painful things of life are real, true, and affect us, we must make a choice daily to focus on the good and to pray for the restoration and healing that only God can work. *We* must choose to move forward with life, even if it's in a new way.

# Chapter 13

## I Was Fired

The days and months to come were still not easy, but I stopped doubting God's plan for us, and I decided to just keep going. I just took it all one day at a time, and I learned more and more to trust that our future would be a good one despite what it looked like. Truthfully, there was nothing easy about it, but God's peace was with me.

I had been working at the studio for a few months by then and doing well. If you recall, Sue's trainer was one of my coworkers, and it was evident that he didn't care much for me. One morning I arrived at the studio at about 4:30 a.m., and the owner was there working out. He was a very kind and laid-back person typically, so when I saw him really getting after it and almost seeming angry as he flipped the oversized tires and sprinted down the walkway with a sled full of weights, I wondered what was wrong. I noticed as I walked by he didn't greet me as he usually did, and that made me feel uneasy. I taught the early morning classes, and everything seemed fine until his wife came into the studio and asked me to meet them both in the classroom after class was over.

The conversation was tense, and I could tell it was one neither of them wanted to have but knew they had to. I could also tell that he was very angry with me, and I'm sure very disappointed.

"Do you have a valid certification?" He asked me, looking me straight in the eyes. The lie I had told that day at the restaurant had finally caught up to me, and despite my best efforts to save enough money to retest and get a current and valid certification since mine had lapsed, I hadn't been able to do so just yet, meaning I was still technically an uncertified trainer working in his facility. I don't think that's what made them the angriest and most disappointed, though; I think it was the fact that I had looked him in the eye that day and lied that made him the most upset and the fact that I had put him and his family at risk for liability, working in his studio without a valid certification.

I owned up to what I had done, explained what my intentions were, and of course, apologized.

"We are going to have to let you go. We will bring you a check for the training that's owed to you and for the percentage that we took out of it. As of today, you are no longer welcome here."

I held myself together as I gathered my items and headed back to my apartment. I had lied, and they had every right to do this to me; I honestly didn't blame them at all. They even told me that if I had just been honest with them, they would have helped pay for my recertification, but I had broken their trust, and there was no repairing that.

They came to the door of my apartment that afternoon and handed me a check for what was owed to me, but also the amount that they could have kept but chose to give to me despite what I had done.

It wasn't a ton of money, but it would be enough to buy me a week or so to figure out what I was going to do next. I gave her a hug and shook his hand, and said, "Thank you, and I'm so sorry."

They wished me good luck and walked away. What on earth would I do next? And how did they find out about my certification? I sat on my living room floor, wallowing in the defeat of my own bad choices once again. I had no place to work. Nowhere to train. No way to make any income. What was I going to do now? I didn't have a valid certification, so no one would hire me. I did still have liability insurance, so if I could just find a private studio that would allow me to pay them a percentage of my profits without the certification, I could work this out. No such luck.

In the meantime, I found out that Sue had been behind the studio owners finding out about my certification. She knew I wasn't currently certified because I had trained at her studio, and I had told her. She told her trainer who worked at the studio I was working at, and sure enough, he let the owners know, knowing full well they would have to let me go.

It could have been very easy for me to play the victim or blame everyone else for what had just happened to me, but the truth was I was the one who lied; I made that choice, and I was reaping the consequences of that choice.

Thank goodness we serve a God who is willing to give us endless chances to continue working things out for our good as we continue to transform. God is so full of mercy, and He sees our hearts. As long as we are willing to change, He's always willing to give us another chance.

I had taken Alex down to my apartment gym with me the next afternoon to get a workout in.

The gym had always been my escape and my happy place. I started asking my mom to take me to the rec center when I was about fourteen years old. I had no clue what I was doing, and no one else in my family was into it, but I had always had a fascination with the human body, with muscles, and lean and healthy-looking physiques. It was something I enjoyed and still do. I believe, in a lot of ways, the gym and working out saved me from choosing other ways to "escape" my pain over the years. I had even competed for years in the profession of physique sports and eventually earned my pro status.

My apartment gym facility was beautiful, brand new, spacious, full of great top-of-the-line equipment, and really was never too busy.

Suddenly I had an idea.

I had been in the apartment for a few months and was an outstanding and helpful tenant who had built some rapport with the staff.

After having a conversation with the complex manager, it was decided; they would allow me to use the facility to train my clients. And even better yet, they would charge me no percentage of my profits!

As long as I was courteous of the other tenants, cleaned up after myself, and didn't do anything "too crazy," she had said, I could use it for free!

I had been paying the other studio that I was fired from 30 percent of my profits to use their facility, and on top of that, I was having to pay for childcare.

And just like that, God had again showed up and showed out, landing me in a beautiful facility that would not only save me 30 percent of my income *but* would also allow me to bring Alex along if I wanted to. Praise God! How gracious and merciful is He that I would lie and sin and fail yet again, and because He knew my heart and He knew what I had going on in my life, He would take a dreadful situation and not only fix it but also use it to promote me even higher.

**Life tip number six: Every challenging circumstance we face in life is an opportunity for God to pull us closer to Him.**

Life will always present challenges and trials. It's easy to say we have faith and that we trust God when things are going well, but it's in those challenging times that God tests us and asks us to cling to Him and believe Him for the solutions. During any trial, we can have peace, and we can choose joy because we know that He has already gone before us and worked it all out on our behalf.

You may be walking in a circumstance right now that looks and feels hopeless. There may look like there is no way out, but I want to encourage you today to run to Him, cling to Him, and trust Him. Use every circumstance you face in life as an opportunity to get closer to Him and to continue growing in your faith.

We must decide to stay steadfast in His promises, believing in who He is and what has already been finished for us. What adventure are you facing today? Don't forget who you are and His love for you, and that you are the only one who can decide what you will or won't do with your adventure.

The apartment gym was great, and between saving the 30 percent I had been paying the studio and saving on childcare since Alex could tag along with me now, I was able to start saving quite a bit of money. I loved our apartment and am forever grateful that we had it for the time that we did, but I also wanted Alex to have a more permanent home. A house with his own yard to play in and settle into.

I knew if that was supposed to happen for us, God would let me know; shoot, he'd already given me a billboard before! I knew if I just kept walking, kept learning, kept changing, and kept trying, God would take me on to our next adventure.

Shane and I had been seeing one another for a while at this point. After about six months or so, I had allowed him to meet Alex; although I did keep a lot of healthy boundaries and kept God and Alex my main priorities, I loved seeing Shane and Alex together. Shane had an almost instantaneous bond and love for Alex. It takes a special man to love a child the way Shane did and always has, and for that, I am so incredibly thankful.

Shane had his own home about twenty minutes from us and, of course, worked full-time as a fireman and first responder. I was working full-time at my apartment complex and with a few in-home clients and some online stuff, plus I was busy chasing after God and being a mama. So, we saw one another and spent as much time together as we possibly could when we were able. Shane was in the midst of his own walk and journey with the Lord and healing. God brought us together at a very inopportune time, but it was in His perfect timing, and soon we would see how He would work through both of us toward a bigger purpose and calling as a couple and as parents.

Shane and I loved hard and fought hard! Truth be told, we still do! Although these days, we are wise enough to know that strife is one of Satan's greatest entries into our lives, so we both know better than to fight or get heated about things now. *But* there were many times in the past when we definitely did!

We are both strong-minded individuals, and being we were both a little older, set in our ways, set in our thinking and routines, not to mention we did every little thing the complete opposite way, it was not an easy road for us. But we did have a strong foundation.

A foundation built on God's Word and promise. And we had a deep passion and love for one another, along with the same vision and goals for life. Neither of us had great examples of godly relationships, love, and marriage, so we were one hundred percent dependent on God to teach us and show us through the Holy Spirit and through His Word.

I once saw an illustration done by Pastor John Hagee, one of my favorite preachers and teachers, regarding marriage, and it has always stuck with me.

> Marriage is like making mashed potatoes. You have two potatoes who enjoy being around one another, talk, laugh, hold hands, and enjoy one another's company. They decide they want to get married and do as the Bible teaches "the two shall become one."
>
> Here are the stages potatoes go through in order to "become one," a.k.a. mashed potatoes.
>
> 1. Step 1; the potato must be peeled. A tearing away of its outer skin/flesh in order to go onto the next steps.
>
> 2. Then comes the boiling. Super-hot boiling water for long periods of time to soften the potato.
>
> 3. Once the potato has been softened, it then gets thrown into a bowl where it is smashed into literal mush and mixed with the other potato.
>
> 4. After a period of smashing, mashing, stirring, and combining, the two potatoes have finally become one substance referred to as mashed potatoes.

Have you ever felt this way in your marriage? I often joke with Shane that even after all these years together, it still sometimes feels like we are only at our peeling stage!

It annoys me to death that he can't leave the thermostat alone for more than five minutes, and he cannot stand how I have to have all of the light switches in their correct on/off positions. I refuse to let him do the dishes because his way is too inefficient, and he can't stand how I constantly move all of his stuff to keep the counters cleared off. But our foundation is strong. The principles and beliefs that we live by and are led by are in line with the Word of God, and we both choose to radically seek God in all that we do. It's okay to not be okay sometimes. It's even okay to feel angry or frustrated. What isn't okay is to decide to stay there in those feelings and circumstances. We must choose love over hate; we must choose forgiveness over pride; we must relinquish the need to be "right" all of the time.

**Life tip number seven: Learn to hate strife more than you love being right!**

If you're married, and you sometimes wonder if you will *ever* get to the point where you've reached the mashed potato phase, cling to the promises of God, cling to one another in Christ, and trust that because of your faithfulness, your marriage is and always will be built on a solid foundation. I am very blessed to have my husband, Shane. He is a good man, and I am forever thankful to have him.

# Chapter 14

## One Day at a Time

There is so much of my day-to-day life back then that I could share. One thing that I really hope you take away from this is that I worked with God. I worked hard. None of my personal journey or transformation was easy, and I still can't say that it's easy. But worth it, yes, one hundred percent yes. I really want you to understand and really get it into your heart that God is only full of goodness for you. He only wants good for you. He is good. He is God. And He has a good plan for your life; if you believe it, receive it, relinquish your own ways for His, and work with Him, I promise you, you will step into so many victories in your life!

Being an entrepreneur for as many years as I have and now being a successful business owner in multiple trades, products, and services, I can tell you that it is absolutely astonishing to me to see the number of people who simply are too lazy to change. I don't know a nicer way to say that. So many people simply don't want to do the work and would rather stay sitting in their misery and not even trying to fulfill their God-given purpose. If you find yourself in that place, now or at any point, realize that the devil is robbing you of your purpose and God's plan for your life by influencing those choices. The devil is very happy with you just sitting and not changing and not working with God to move forward; in fact, the devil is thrilled to see you doing that. You may be saved. You may be going to heaven, but what are you doing for God while you are here? The devil wants nothing more than for you to miss that.

So rather than choosing to allow the devil's hold on you and your life and your purpose, how about you decide right now that you are no longer going to give the devil that kind of power in your life? How about you decide right now that, with God, *all things are possible* and that you can do all things through Him who is your strength? Will it be easy? No. It won't.

Can you do it with Him, and grow, and get stronger, and change, and learn, and be influential, and make an impact in this world for Jesus? One hundred percent yes, you can.

"Poor is he who works with a negligent and idle hand, But the hand of the diligent makes him rich" (Proverbs 10:4).

"The soul (appetite) of the lazy person craves and gets nothing [for lethargy overcomes ambition], But the soul (appetite) of the diligent [who works willingly] is rich and abundantly supplied" (Proverbs 13:4).

If you're making this choice today, I want you to send me an email and tell me.

Yes, right now, make the choice and send me an email to jennybishopcoach@gmail.com that says, "I have decided to give the devil a big black eye today!" Tell me what you are going to do and what you are going to be working on! I will be praying for you wholeheartedly and believing in God's miraculous power, wisdom, and strength in your life!

Alex and I were in the apartment for about two years. I had been able to take that 30 percent I was saving from not having to pay any rental fees and had started a decent down payment.

And then came the next miracle in my life, miss Becky. Becky had come to me as a client, and we had grown close. She had a daughter named Jen, ironically enough, who struggled with drug addiction, and Becky had a lot of negativity in her life as a result. Her husband, Ray, was a wealthy businessman. Becky and I had great talks. Talks about life, talks about family, and of course, talks about God. Becky had self admittedly turned away from God at some point in her life. Sometimes when people don't really understand who God is or how He works, it's easy to place blame on Him when disaster strikes. Slowly but surely, Becky would listen to me "preaching," sharing God's truth and Word, not to mention she was seeing firsthand the miracles He was working for Alex and me, and that could not be denied. I had shared my hopes to find a house for Alex and me, and it just so happened that in the neighborhood right across the street from our apartment, there was a perfect house that had hit the market. It needed a little TLC for sure, but hey, you know I have zero issues with hard work. The three-bedroom, two-bathroom home was built the year I was born, 1978. It was a split-level home, so Alex and I would have plenty of space upstairs, and downstairs could be used as my very own in-home workout studio. To be honest, I could not have come up with a better scenario. In conversation, one day, Becky asked me about it. I wanted the house, but I had just been on my own and working again for two years, and the down payment... well, I was about nine thousand dollars short on that. Then one day, when she had come for her workout, "I talked to Ray, and we would like to give you that nine thousand dollars. We would also like to help you fix it up, help you get your studio equipment, and redo that old driveway."

Yep. That happened. I, a wretched sinner, just kept having miracles sent my way. I, a disgrace, kept having people planted in my life. I, a complete screwup, was about to buy my very own house for my son and me. After two years of struggle, uncertainty, too many sleepless nights to count, tears, illness, and fear, here God had put this woman in my life who was willing and able to help me. And that she did. And Alex and I had an official home.

Becky, when you read this, I want you to know that I will never forget what you did for Alex and me, and I am forever grateful and indebted to you for it. Love you!

Here's the thing. Two years prior to meeting Becky, I had no way of knowing that she would come into my life. I had no way of knowing things were going to work out. I had no way of knowing God's exact plan; what I did know was that He did have a good plan for me because that's what His Word tells me. But had I relied on what I knew, on what I could see, or on what I could understand, then I would have never stepped into that miracle and into that victorious place He had prepared for me. I would have stayed comfortable! Miserable but comfortable, and I would have missed it all! As a matter of fact, if I hadn't taken the leap that day and pulled out of that driveway, and never gone back, I wouldn't be writing this book today. I wouldn't have met Shane. We wouldn't have our youngest son, Ashton. Life would be very different. I shudder just thinking of this. I love my life so much. I love God so much. I love what God has done, and I am so thankful I decided to do the work with Him.

Sit and ponder this for a minute. What are you *not* doing because you can't see how it will work out? Where are you not going because you can't understand? What are you staying in that you know you shouldn't because you don't know how to do anything else?

Step out. Find out. Keep going. Trust God.

Shall we pray together for a moment? Repeat this prayer:

> Father, I come to You today knowing that I am a mess without You. I am unsure of my exact direction. I am unsure of the exact plan You have for my life, but I know You do have one and that it is a good plan. God, I want to work with You. I want

You to lead my life in every way. Please help me surrender all that I know of myself and all that I don't know to You so that You can work. Please help me resist the devil and tell him to get lost. Please help me make choices to stay close to You. I ask for Your wisdom, Father, Your strength, Your courage, and Your guidance, and today I declare that I am doing things Your way. I thank You for everything that is already finished for me, and I am walking with You until I step into the victories that You have planned for my life. Jesus, I'm forever grateful for Your love and sacrifice. Amen.

# Chapter 15

## Loving Others

This chapter may surprise you a bit. Most people associate loving others with just rolling over and taking any kind of treatment from people. Or many people say things like, "Well, it's not my place to judge; I'm not perfect either, so we will just let it go."

Sometimes we mix up having grace with permitting habitual bad behavior. It's one thing to make a mistake once or maybe even a couple of times. But what we all need to understand is that when the person's behavior does not change, and the same patterns are repeated over and over again for months or even years, this person has truly not repented, not come fully to Jesus, and has not changed. Do you know that when you don't call this person out, when you decide to "just keep the peace" or continue allowing this mediocrity in your life, you're not only allowing the devil to steal that individual's plan for their life, but you are also allowing the devil to steal yours?

**Life tip number eight: You cannot allow long-term habitual bad behavior or sin into your life through yourself or from someone else, no matter who that person is or what you feel your responsibility is to them.**

Let's park here for a minute and look at some scriptures because it doesn't really matter at all what I have to say about this subject; what matters is what God says about this subject.

And truth be told, sometimes loving others means you walk away, and yes, even let them know in love that the way they are living is not the way they should be living.

If you are facing a decision about a situation such as this, be sure to get into the Word for yourself. Meditate on these scriptures, and ask God to reveal to you what He wants you to do.

We should never seek our plan for our life, only His plans. And if you ask Him to guide you and lead you and give you the courage to do things He may ask you to do, He will. God will never leave you nor forsake you, and God will never fail you.

So how can you know if a behavior or behaviors line up with the Word of God?

"Blessed [fortunate, prosperous, and favored by God] is the man who does not walk in the counsel of the wicked [following their advice and example], nor stand in the path of sinners, nor sit [down to rest] in the seat of scoffers (ridiculers)" (Psalm 1:1).

"He who walks [as a companion] with wise men will be wise, But the companions of [conceited, dull-witted] fools [are fools themselves and] will experience harm" (Proverbs 13:20).

> No temptation [regardless of its source] has overtaken or enticed you that is not common to human experience [nor is any temptation unusual or beyond human resistance]; but God is faithful [to His word—He is compassionate and trustworthy], and He will not let you be tempted beyond your ability [to resist], but along with the temptation He [has in the past and is now and] will [always] provide the way out as well, so that you will be able to endure it [without yielding, and will overcome temptation with joy].

1 Corinthians 10:13

"Do not be unequally bound together with unbelievers [do not make mismatched alliances with them, inconsistent with your faith]. For what partnership can righteousness have with lawlessness? Or what fellowship can light have with darkness?" (2 Corinthians 6:14).

"Take care, brothers and sisters, that there not be in any one of you a wicked, unbelieving heart [which refuses to trust and rely on the Lord, a heart] that turns away from the living God" (Hebrews 3:12).

Most people are too afraid to hold people accountable to God's Word because they may get offended or upset. What we all need to realize is that we should be more concerned with what God has called us to do and with doing it than we should be about how other people will think, feel, or react. And yes, sometimes this can mean having to have a conversation that is extremely uncomfortable or having to draw boundaries that are painful. Your focus needs to stay steadfast on God's Word. Stay focused on what He tells you to do, and stay focused on His plan for you. Fulfilling the life God has for you should trump anything else in your life. And I want you to keep in mind that if God tells you to do something, if He asks you to stand up or asks you to say something, or if He asks you to cut something or someone out of your life, then He will give you the courage, strength, understanding, and peace to do so.

If someone is mistreating you, God does not expect you to stay in close relationship with them. As a matter of fact, as I showed you in the scriptures above, having that influence closely in your life can inhibit your blessings from God. Love them, yes. Pray for them, yes. Forgive them, yes. Hope the very best for them, yes. But do they need to stay in close relationship with you if they are refusing to seek God in their own choices and truly repent, turn away from their own sin, and go a new way? Does God expect that? No.

When I was about sixteen or seventeen years old, my mother held a gun to her head right in front of me and told me she was going to make me watch. Of course, at that time, I was convinced it was all my fault that she chose to act this way. I was the worst teenager; I gave her such a hard time; she just couldn't take any more of what I was doing; she had no other choice than to act in that way because nothing else was working. These were among some of the continuous things I had heard from her.

Back up about six or seven years; I was about nine, and my brother about seven. We were both in bed, sound asleep, when my dad came in and woke us and told us to go sit out on the couch. You can imagine our confusion; it was the middle of the night, and we had zero clue what was going on.

Out of the dark hallway came my mom. Screaming at the top of her lungs and waving a belt around. My brother and I ducked and covered as she started in on us with the belt. My dad, well, he just stood there. Don't ask me how long it was; I have no clue. It might have been thirty seconds, or it might have been five minutes. I really don't recall. But does that matter?

It was long enough for the belt buckle to break my hand open and for it to start bleeding.

My dad picked me up and took me to the bathroom. He set me on the counter and started to rinse off my hand. I could tell he was upset, but the words he chose to use were, "Look what you made your mother do."

Now let's fast forward to 2014. I am a grown woman in my thirties with my own child. My mom lost her temper yet again and chose to hit me in the face. And when she told my dad, "Well, I hit her," his response was, "Well, good."

Do you see a pattern here? Do you see habitual behaviors that are not being influenced by God? Was life this way *all of the time*? No, it wasn't. But does that matter?

This behavior not only has never changed after all of these years, but there have never even been apologies made. As a matter of fact, the blame, last I knew, was still placed on me. It was always my fault, my brother's fault, or my dad's fault that my mom acted the way she did.

Even when I was going to see Bonnie, even still today, my tendency is to protect my mom. Even though I know that the choices she made for herself and our family were not okay, I somehow always find myself saying something like, "Well, it wasn't always bad. I would say 80 percent of the time things were okay; it was just that 20 percent that was bad and not just a little bad, off the hook crazy bad!"

When there is no repentance and continual, habitual, ungodly behavior, that opens doors for Satan and his army to walk right into your life and the life of those around you. That is not a chance you should be willing to take, and God does not expect you to.

The word "repent," which was used by John the Baptist, Jesus, and Peter, is the Greek word *metanoeo*. This word means "a decision to completely change or to entirely turn around in the way one is thinking, believing, or living; a total transformation wholly affecting every part of a person's life, including their behavior."

People can ask for forgiveness all day long, maybe even acknowledge what they did was wrong (that is not the case with my parents, unfortunately), but if the behavior habitually continues over long periods of time, then it's safe to say they have not truly repented or made the decision to turn away from the sin and work with God to change.

Your situation may not look like mine, but perhaps you have a friend who has bad language or uses the Lord's name in vain often. You may not think it's your place to say anything to them, but the truth is, if you love them and want God's best for them, you have a responsibility to actually tell them; if you don't say anything to them and they continue in that behavior, they are blocking their own blessings from God.

And please let us not forget, while we are taking an inventory of everyone else's behaviors and actions, that we need to always be aware of our own. While you pray for God to change the hearts and minds of others, be sure to ask Him to be doing the same for you.

There is a scripture that is used often out of context and is confusing for some regarding this issue:

"Do not judge and criticize and condemn [others unfairly with an attitude of self-righteous superiority as though assuming the office of a judge], so that you will not be judged [unfairly]" (Matthew 7:1).

This scripture is referring to judging others in a self-righteous way. Meaning you're judging their bad behavior while you are actually committing the same or similar bad behaviors yourself, but you are deceived into thinking your bad behavior is okay.

In more simple terms, don't be a hypocrite.

Let me wrap up this chapter with this. As true followers of Christ, we should all live with certain standards in our lives. That doesn't mean anyone is better or worse than anyone else; it just means that there is a standard you live by based on God's Word, and part of that standard is a commandment to love people, and sometimes loving people means telling them hard truths so that they can have the opportunity, like you have had as well, to repent and receive all of the blessing that God has for them and their life.

# Chapter 16

## You Have an Enemy

**M**y next life tip, number nine, is that you need to understand that God is not in control of everything!

One of the most difficult things to explain to non-believers, or even believers who are fairly new in their journey with the Lord, is why do bad things happen. Why does God allow bad things to happen to people if He loves them so much?

For me, I could have chosen to have a "woe to me attitude":

Why did God allow me to be sexually abused starting at the age of three?

Why did God give me a family full of dysfunction?

Why didn't God change things for us?

My husband could use the following:

Why did my biological father abandon me?

Why was my biological father an alcoholic?

Why didn't God give me a good dad?

Or how about any of these:

Why does God allow for children to get sick?

Why does God allow natural disasters?

Why does God allow people in power to rise and then murder

thousands of people?

Let's face it; this list could go on and on and on.

Something I have learned that may surprise you a bit is that God is *not* in control of everything.

God is the Alpha and the Omega, the beginning and the end. There will one hundred percent come a time when every knee will bow, and every human will declare Jesus is Lord. There will one hundred percent come a time when good will prevail eternally over evil. There will one hundred percent come a time of the millennial reign where we (believers) get to live on this earth for one thousand years in complete peace.

There is a God, a triune, all-knowing, all-powerful God Almighty, that is in control of the entire outcome, *but* He is not in control of everything.

I remember a conversation I had in the parking lot of the second gym that I owned in Elizabeth, Colorado, with my then business partner. After embarking into this business partnership and opening the gym facility, I found out he was an atheist and his wife, well, I think she believed, but regardless we were definitely unequally yoked.

I had just gotten in my H2 Hummer to head to a Joyce Meyer conference and had left the gym early that day to do so. He had followed me into the parking lot and said to me, "If your God is real, then why do bad things happen? How does a good and loving God exist, and such horrible things happen every single day?"

This was before I was on my radical journey with Jesus, but I mustered up the only answer I could think of at that time, "Bad things happen because of people, not because of God. Bad things happen because Satan is an influencer in this world."

I remember he scoffed at me and walked off.

That business partnership didn't last long, to say the least. Do yourself a favor and listen to God when He tells you in His Word not to be in close relationship with people you are unequally yoked with.

I found out about a year ago that man ended up taking his own life.

Do you recall what happened in the garden of Eden? Eve was deceived, and Adam made a choice to follow. A decision. A choice.

God *gave* man the ability to choose. He said to Adam, "You may eat of any tree in this garden except the tree of the knowledge of good and evil, for if you eat of that tree, you will surely die." (Referring to a spiritual death.)

Again, Satan, as the great deceiver he is, deceived Eve, and she was persuaded to eat the fruit. But Adam, Adam had a clear, logical choice to make. And he chose. And he ate. And God did not stop him from making that decision, nor did He interfere.

You and I have an enemy on this earth. Referred to as the "god of this world" in 2 Corinthians 4:4, "among them the god of this world [Satan] has blinded the minds of the unbelieving to prevent them from seeing the illuminating light of the gospel of the glory of Christ, who is the image of God."

When the fall occurred, power of this earth was turned over to Satan himself.

In Matthew 4:9, Satan said to Jesus, "All these things I will give You, if You fall down and worship me." Speaking of all of the kingdoms of the world.

If Satan wasn't the god of this world, a.k.a. an enemy here on earth, then why would he have the ability to give away all of the kingdoms of the world?

Satan is here, and he is here to do one thing and one thing only: to kill, steal, and destroy.

To inflict pain, to afflict with illness and disease, to cause division and strife, to deceive and lead people away from God, to influence prideful and selfish hearts and minds. He is prowling like a lion, just waiting for someone that he can devour. He seeks those that will yield to him and his ways and his influence so that he can indeed kill, steal, and destroy.

When that drunk individual makes a choice to get into his or her car and drive home, and then that car crashes and kills someone, it is because of that choice that individual made. God had nothing to do with that choice, nor did God want that to happen, but God will never interfere with someone's free will.

When I was sexually abused for the first time at the age of three years old, that was because a human was under the influence of Satan and his plan to destroy me. God had nothing to do with that, God did not want that to happen, but God would not interfere with that individual's choices.

When my mom held a gun to her head and told me she was "going to make me watch," God had nothing to do with that. My mom was yielding to the influence of Satan and Satan's plan to destroy us both. God was there, but He did not interfere with her right to choose.

Do you see how serious this is? Do you see that this earth is flooded with the influence of the great deceiver and evil one?

You'd better do yourself a favor and write this one down and keep it, and meditate on it, and *do it* daily in your life: "So submit to [the authority of] God. Resist the devil [stand firm against him] and he will flee from you" (James 4:7).

Submit—step one. Resist—Step two. Got that?

Let's break that down;

"Submit" means "come to God daily willing to relinquish all that you are in the flesh for all that He is and all that He has for you." This doesn't have to look like some "big-deal," magical thing. Again, God sees your heart. A simple "Well, here I am again today, God, I ask you to reveal to me what needs to be revealed. Give me eyes to see and ears to hear, and help me change into who you created me to be. I submit all that I am to you. Now help me!"

"Resist" means a couple of different things to me. Using my authority in Jesus, and yes, speaking out loud in Jesus' name and telling the devil that he is not welcome in my life or in my home, and he can just get lost. It also means that I need to pay attention to how I act and what I say when the trials of life come at me. If I succumb to ungodly behavior during difficult times, then I'm giving the devil an open invitation to walk right into my life. So even when he tries to come after me, I can recognize and know what he is up to; I can then tell him to get lost, and at the same time stay in peace, choose joy and love, and I tell you what, the devil has zero power or victory when you do that!

Now let's check out the second part of this scripture: "So submit to [the authority of] God. Resist the devil [stand firm against him] and he will flee from you. Come close to God [with a contrite heart] and He will come close to you. Wash your hands, you sinners; and purify your [unfaithful] hearts, you double-minded [people]" (James 4:7–8).

"Clean up your lives, you sinners"—obviously, He is speaking to those who are unsaved when He says, "you sinners."

Do you walk around calling yourself a sinner? If you have accepted Christ into your heart, then for heaven's sake, please stop calling yourself a sinner, because you have Christ in you, which means you are no longer a sinner. That is no longer who you are. You are now a new creature in Christ Jesus, who is your strength.

Now, do we sin? Of course we sin! But just as I tell my children, your behavior is not who you are. It is simply what you do. And what you do can change and be molded into who you are in Christ because Christ will enable that change when it's accompanied by your acknowledgment and willingness.

The next part of the scripture states, "purify your heart, you people who can't make up your mind."

Are you in? Or are you out? Are you for God? Or are you against Him? Are you serving yourself, or are you serving God in all that you do?

*Or* are you at least trying and aware of where you fall short, but you are willing to change?

This part of the scripture is basically telling all of us to stop being double-minded. To stop accepting standards that don't line up with God's Word. To stop being a "lukewarm" Christian and be all-in with God. The more you genuinely pursue God and choose to put Him first, the closer He will come to you, which in turn will reflect in your heart, your choices, your behaviors, and the fruits of your life.

If you're a believer in Christ, you need not fear our enemy that's loose in the world. Although he does have power and influence here, he does *not* have any authority over us. When you're in the family of God as a believer in Jesus Christ, believing that He was God in the flesh who came down to make the ultimate sacrifice to fulfill the law and relieve you of it by simply believing and confessing that He did so, then you now have authority over Satan.

"Listen carefully: I have given you authority [that you now possess] to tread on serpents and scorpions, and [the ability to exercise authority] over all the power of the enemy (Satan); and nothing will [in any way] harm you" (Luke 10:19).

*Use your authority!* Tell Satan to get lost! Submit your life to Christ, repent for what you need to repent for, and work with God to change and go a new way, but also you will need to learn to exercise your authority over Satan because the stronger you grow in your relationship with Christ, the stronger he will come against you.

Pray over yourself. Pray over your home and your family. Use your power in Jesus. Use your authority in Jesus. Make Satan scared of *you* because of who you are in Him!

"The weapons of our warfare are not physical [weapons of flesh and blood]. Our weapons are divinely powerful for the destruction of fortresses" (2 Corinthians 10:4).

# Chapter 17

## Wonder Woman

My house was beautiful, and I loved it so much. Alex was doing so well; things were good.

Really good.

Each morning I would wake up and walk down my hallway, the sun shining through the front windows, feeling overwhelmed with gratitude.

I had a full book of clients, and although the schedule was demanding, my studio was inside my house, so there wasn't much to complain about.

Alex spent his days hanging out with me, playing; we enjoyed our walks over to Shillito Park, which was right around the corner, and catching lightning bugs. I was actually doing a good job as a mama. Alex was loved. Safe. Happy. Secure. He had never been harmed in any way.

That was all I cared about.

Shane and I, of course, were still dating and getting more serious. If you're reading this and you aren't married yet, I have a piece of advice to give. Date with a purpose. Do not just date to date. Date with an intention in mind, and if you find out quickly the individual does not meet your desires for a forever companion, then stop dating them! Dating isn't supposed to be for fun and games; it's supposed to be purposeful.

Our relationship was far from perfect, still is. But there was an attraction between us that kept us together, and it was way more than a physical attraction. We both had big dreams, goals, and visions for our life, and they were not only material things, but we also both had a burning desire to change. To live victorious lives that were purposeful.

Some of my favorite memories of Shane and me in our early dating years were the times I would go to his house, and he would cook us dinner. It would take him at least two hours to cook the meal (he is a great cook, though), and then we'd eat and sit and talk for hours and hours.

Our talks always revolved around life and purpose, and we became best friends.

Christmas time was coming, Shane's absolute favorite time of the year. We had put his Christmas tree up early that year, and Alex and I headed down for a nice evening at Shane's house. It was always peaceful and relaxing at Shane's. Shane's greatest gift is his ability to serve. He truly loves to serve people, so, needless to say, when I went to his house, Alex and I were basically waited on hand and foot. We ate a nice meal, watched some good ole Christmas shows, and I was curled up cozy on the couch. Alex was playing on the floor when Shane said to me, "Hey, I want you to come check out this ornament; I got it just for you."

Reluctant to leave my cozy slumber, I replied, "Well, can't you just bring it here?"

We went back and forth a couple of times when I finally got up with a sigh of irritation.

The ornament was a Wonder Woman ornament tied to the tree branch by a little yellow ribbon.

(*He really made me get up and come over here for this?* I thought to myself.)

"Honey, it's super cute, thank you!" I turned to head back to the couch.

"I think you're missing something," he said. "You need to look closer."

What was he talking about? I went back over and examined the ornament again, but this time a little closer. And there it was. The twinkling Christmas lights reflecting in the clear white stones.

"That's a ring!" I exclaimed quickly removing the ornament and maneuvering the ring from the tied ribbon.

And down on one knee with Alex by his side, next to our Christmas tree, Shane asked me to marry him.

We were so full of joy and excitement! Such a memorable moment!

After the initial excitement wore off a bit, we then, of course, started making the calls to family and friends to share the news. His mom and dad (Billy and Judy) were elated as well as the rest of his family.

Billy and Judy have been such a blessing to our family and to me; I always say I lucked out in the in-law department.

Before I called my parents, Shane asked me, "Are you sure you want to call them now?"

My husband has a God-given gift of discernment. I mean, he never gets it wrong; when he feels something about people or about a situation, he nails it every time.

"Yea, I'm sure! I just want to tell them." I responded to him.

I excitedly dialed the number. Things still weren't great with my parents, but I was still trying to make something work.

After sharing the news, there was a dead silence on the line. "Mom, are you there?"

Still silence. "Hello?"

It was like the balloon had been totally full and ready to be tied up, and then it got a slow leak...leak...leak, and then, "Ok. Well, what do you want me to say?" she replied in a stale, hasty tone. Want to hear something crazy? In that moment, I realized something about myself.

I was familiar with this reaction and this tone from my mom, and even though I hadn't realized it before, it actually affected me physically. I looked down at my hand, and it was literally trembling. I could feel my blood pressure was up; my entire body was now shaking. A defense response is what I've learned this is. When you've had the same type of incident or abuse happen repeatedly, your body develops a defensive response, and that is what was happening.

I realized something else in that moment as well; the "nicey-nice" facade my mom had been putting on over recent months was just that, a facade. There was no real change. Here we were again, back where we always got to.

"Well, I don't know, maybe you could say congratulations? That you're happy for me or any of those things?"

Shane was looking at me across the kitchen. "Just hang up," he said.

Words got heated, there was a short exchange, and then my mom just hung up on me.

And there I was, shaking from head to toe and in tears. And just like that, the joy we had ten minutes before that call had been completely sucked out of the room.

Shane was angry. He had never really gotten angry over my

parents before. He had just let me make my choices and supported me in them, but this time was different.

In a calm but assertive way, he approached me and said, "Jenny, you can do what you want, but for me, I will not have that in my life, and you should love yourself enough not to allow it either."

I remember Bonnie asking me one time, "Why is it that you want this person in your life so badly?"

"Because she's my mom," I replied through tears.

What I've had to accept and embrace is that it doesn't matter who it is; if their relationship presents a toxic and repetitive situation, you cannot allow it into close proximity of your life.

If you do, you give the enemy an entry, as we went over before, but also, if you keep allowing it, then God never has the opportunity to work with that person on change. You become an enabler.

Be smart and prayerful in this decision if you are facing one. Wait on God to guide you, whether that's through a person or circumstance or just something you feel Him say. Once you've received clarity, decide and stick to it, and do not compromise peace in your life.

I am not saying it is easy; it is not. One day at a time, one prayer at a time.

We are never without hope in Jesus.

# Chapter 18

## Ashton

We got married at the end of October. My in-laws helped me plan and execute the most perfectly amazing day. Billy and Judy, I love you, and I'm so thankful for you.

Perfect weather, perfect setting, perfect everything. It was intimate and peaceful, and that was what we wanted. A time for us to be in front of God, declaring this commitment and love for one another. Alex was with me as I walked down the aisle. Shane and I wrote our vows and meant them. The Lord was there that day in those perfect fluffy clouds surrounded by big blue skies.

We all danced and laughed through the night, and then Shane and I departed in an incredible 1970ish Turquoise Chevelle. (Anyone else into old classic cars?)

A lot of people have asked me over the years if I have any regret about no one from my biological family being there that day. My answer is simple. That day was about God, Shane, and me. It was peaceful, beautiful, and momentous. I have no regrets and believe it was as it was supposed to be.

Life certainly didn't stop after this wonderful day. We had a lot happening. We needed to sell Shane's house, had to move all three of us into my house, and about a month after our wedding, we found out I was pregnant!

We decided to try right away, we knew we wanted more kiddos, and Alex was getting older, not to mention we were getting older as well.

Our sweet, sweet Ashton Jacob, a.k.a. "Ashy-boy," was born on August 4, 2017. The delivery was fast and furious, and once again, despite the health issues that I faced, he was perfect, and all was well.

Alex embraced the big brother role and still does. How cool is it to watch little humans that you get to bring into the world grow and learn and change? There is just nothing else like it!

Ashton has always just been happy. Always smiling and always the one to lighten up a moody room. He will also tell you like it is, for example, "Well, Mom, really what you said was not very nice, and you really, really should say you're sorry and not do that again."

Our boys. They bring us our greatest joys and yet some of our greatest challenges.

This life will bring you pain and loss and joy and triumph. It will showcase the pleasures of life and love and also the power of letting go and moving into new seasons. The boys have taught me so much. And I know there is still much to come.

Shane and I knew, at some point, the conversation about my family would come up; it was only a matter of time. While driving in the car one day, Alex asked me, "Hey, Mom, do you have a mom and a dad? Or any brothers or sisters?" That day on the car ride home, I got to tell my boys about their grandparents and their uncle, whom they don't remember, and one has never met. Their names, where they live, and what they do, and I even shared some good stories and memories about them.

When they ask why we don't talk, I am honest with them. I let them know as things stand, it wouldn't be good for our family, but we can stay hopeful that one day it can be healthy, and if not, we can see them all in heaven one day.

# Chapter 19

## The Undercurrent

Our flesh is strong. I like to refer to it as our undercurrent. It is filled with ego, pride, our own will, our own desires, our own ideas, our own opinions, and our own thoughts. I think you get the point.

Have you ever read the scripture in Matthew where Jesus Himself said, "Many are called, but few are chosen"?

Jesus often spoke in parables, and in this specific parable, He spoke about a wedding. A king had sent invitations for this wedding, but the people who received them did not come because they were too busy "doing their own thing." When the king heard this, he became angry and sent his people back out, saying to invite anyone off of the streets who wanted to attend, and the wedding became full of guests.

Truth be told, every one of us was created by God for a purpose, on purpose, and with a purpose, and we are all *called* to it. So why are so many people miserable, unfulfilled, and living without victory in their lives? And yes, that included Christians.

Referring to the parable, the people who were invited were not willing to go because they were too busy doing their own thing. Are you doing your own thing? Or are you doing God's thing?

I wasted so many years doing my own thing. Going around the same mountains. Landing in the same messes. Spinning in the same confusions.

So, if we all have been called, why are so few chosen? And chosen does not refer to your salvation; let me be clear about that. If you've decided that Jesus is your Lord and Savior, then your salvation is not in question here. Chosen refers to the following: are you living in the purpose and fulfillment that God created you for? Are you really living in that? Or are you living in "your own thing?"

Here are a few things for you to ponder as you seek this answer:

- Are you filled with spirit-filled joy that overflows out of you every day?

- Do you look forward to and enjoy the things you're spending your life doing?

- Do the things you do come naturally for you?

- Do you rest easy at night?

- Are you able to maintain spiritual peace despite what's happening around you?

- How's your mood?

OR

- Do you dread the things you're doing or spending your time on?

- Do you lay awake at night wondering if you can make it through another day or if this is all there is to life?

- Do you feel deep down that you were made for more?

- Do you desire more than you have? Whether that be financial, spiritual, or relational.

- How's your mood?

In Matthew 12:33–37, Jesus teaches how our words reveal our character. "For the mouth speaks out of that which fills the heart" (Matthew 12:34).

This is why I think it is imperative to really see how our mood is. That is our undercurrent.

Sure, mood basically means what you say, think, and feel, which is your soul and emotions. But if this mood and undercurrent are habitually off track and repeatedly producing the same fruits in your life, then maybe you really need to take a deeper look at the health of your spirit. Maybe you really need to spend time in prayer and dig deep with the Holy Spirit, asking Him to reveal to you what the issues may be.

Many times, this undercurrent has been affected by circumstances, past experiences, or other people, but what if I presented you with the idea that your undercurrent could also be affected negatively because you truly are not living within your spiritual God-given purpose?

I like to think of this as a spiritual clash. If you have two cymbals, one cymbal represents your spirit living within your God-given purpose, and the other represents you "doing your own thing" in and with your life. And listen, maybe your "own thing" is working out okay for you. Maybe everyone around you approves. Maybe you have money, things, influence. *But* are you happy? Are you fulfilled inside? If you are, then may God's plan continue in your life and continue to bless you. But, if that is not you, and you are unhappy and unfulfilled and oftentimes wondering why in the world you are here on this earth, then I want you to understand that, most likely, there is a clash going on inside of you. All day. Every day. Cymbal 1 and Cymbal 2 are smacking into each other and creating a whole lot of loud, obnoxious, and exhausting noise.

This is because even though Cymbal 2 may be paying your bills or maybe it is the thing that all of your loved ones approve of or want you to do, it doesn't really matter at all if it's clashing with Cymbal 1, which is God's divine purpose for you and your life.

I am not telling you to do anything irresponsible or put yourself or your family in a bad situation to go after your purpose. But what I am saying is, *work on it!* If God truly has called you to something, He will help you get there. It will not look like a magic wand, and poof, everything just happens, but if you go to Him, stick with Him, and follow Him, He will make a way, and He will help because He does want you to live within that divine purpose that He Himself created you for.

I love listening to my husband talk with people. When we moved to Texas in 2018, he had just retired from the Lexington Fire Department, and to be honest, he wasn't really sure what his next chapter in life would be as far as work was concerned.

So, he tried a lot of things. My husband is a person of excellence, and boy, does he work! He tried retail; he tried the food business; he tried retail again. And even though some paid well, and he was in leadership roles, he would come home and tell me, "Babe, it's just not me." He knew that inside of him, there was a terrible clash happening.

So we prayed and prayed, and I laid awake at night wondering what God might have in store for Shane and what it was He wanted me to do for Shane, if anything. And one day, we just decided to take the leap of faith that we felt God had told us to do; Shane quit his last job and came home. And we sat, and we waited. And we prayed. And we waited. And it was hard. And we had enough, but it was hard. And then, one day, not too long after this leap of faith, three opportunities presented themselves within a two-week time frame, and just like that, Shane was working a mile up the street, volunteering and speaking at church, and being propelled into a new sales position that he could work from home and had the flexibility and income potential that we desired.

I heard Shane on a Zoom call with one of the leaders in the company one day. The man was going on and on about the company's income and earnings and about that potential. Shane very calmly said, "I can appreciate that, but just so you know, I am not about the money. I never have been, and I never will be. I am about the purpose and the intent, and whatever results from that is fine with me, no matter what it equates to." I am pretty sure that man had never had someone say that to him before, because it seemed for a moment that he was a bit speechless.

Matthew 7:7–8 states, "Ask and keep on asking and it will be given to you; seek and keep on seeking and you will find; knock and keep on knocking and the door will be opened to you. For everyone who keeps on asking receives, and he who keeps on seeking finds, and to him who keeps on knocking, it will be opened."

How many of us have heard the first part of this scripture more than once? "Ask and keep on asking and it will be given to you."

I know that I have heard it many times.

But how many times have you heard, read, or meditated on the rest? "Seek and keep on seeking and you will find; knock and keep on knocking and the door will be opened to you."

See, we can all ask God all day, every day, for what we want. But what the prayer should really be is, "God, please reveal to me what you want for me."

And then, once He's revealed that to you, once you've asked, it then says you have to seek and knock.

Seek Him. Which means get into His Word and live by it.

Seek direction, seek wisdom, seek guidance. The kind that only comes from His Word and through the Holy Spirit. Do you realize the man whom the Bible states was the wisest man, Solomon, asked God for His wisdom? Of all of the things he could have asked for, his only request to God was for God to give him wisdom.

That should be pretty telling to us when it comes to what we ask for from God.

And then it tells us to knock. I don't know about you, but in order to knock, that means you must do something, right? It takes action to knock.

You can pray, and ask, and seek, but when you do so, be ready because, most likely, there will be something that God asks you to do. Some type of action.

We did not know how things would work out when Shane quit his job; however, we both knew that Cymbal 1 and Cymbal 2 were clashing and that the fruit of that was spilling over into our lives. We both knew that God was telling us that He did not want Shane there. We sought God's guidance, and then we knocked. We started asking around, we started being more aware of opportunities around us, and to be one hundred percent honest, God sent one person right through our front door that would lead us to speak at our church, which fills our Cymbal 1 like nothing else does!

God can only work when we work with Him. He can only bless us when we do our part. He can only move mountains when we surrender our will.

Purpose does not mean easy, but it does mean peace.

And once you reach that point, you will find that the loud, obnoxious, and exhausting noise that once was is now replaced with peace, joy, and fulfillment. The kind that only your

God-given purpose can give.

The majority of people in the world today have this way of living completely backward.

Most think that having it all "together" with their health and bodies, finances, relationships, worldly status, and influence will then lead them to feelings of joy and fulfillment and bring them spiritual peace.

Most people truly believe that outward things will fulfill their inward desires and purpose.

This is backward entirely. We are all spiritual beings at our core. So, we all need to start there. The spiritual God-given purpose will enable all of the other things in your soul, body, and outward life that will all lead to the fulfillment and joy most are missing.

Let's walk through this:

God enables us through His Holy Spirit to discover and step into the purpose that He created us for.

It is from that place of purpose, which is revealed to us through our spirit, that we find fulfillment in our human nature because our spirit has been filled first, which then causes our soul (mind, will, emotions) to feel things such as happiness, excitement, motivation, peace, inspiration, which then comes out of our physical bodies in the form of what God refers to as fruit. A fruitful life directed by our Creator.

So basically, if we could just turn everyone who's born again inside out, then we'd all just be doing fabulous. Work at this. Because you do not want to get to the end of your life here on this earth, which we all will eventually, and be so far off from what God had planned for you.

The best news about all of this is that it is completely doable!

You can change your undercurrent, your mood, your circumstances, and your life. You can take what you are learning here and apply it, and you will make progress and start moving in the right direction. That is something to be excited about!

**Life tip number ten: A fulfilled spirit leads to a joyful body and life. A fulfilled spirit enables the soul and body to experience health and abundant joy and peace. Fulfill your spirit first; the rest will follow.**

"Hope deferred makes the heart sick, but when desire is fulfilled, it is a tree of life" (Proverbs 13:12).

"Many are the plans in a person's heart, but it is the Lord's purpose that prevails" (Proverbs 19:21, NIV).

# Chapter 20

## Are You in Denial?

You all know this word; I am certain of it. Have you ever sat down with God and asked Him if there are areas in which you are in denial? If so, have you listened to what He reveals to you?

I don't know if any of you have certain times or scenarios in your day where you feel like you hear the voice of the Lord a little louder than at other times of the day, but for me, there are a couple of times that I can hear more clearly and more often, and one of those times is in the middle of the night, which, I'll be honest, sometimes gets a little challenging because I really need my sleep, if you know what I mean. This tends to happen for me in chunks of time, meaning a solid one- or two-week period where He's waking me up around 2 or 3 a.m. I've learned to just get up and go into my office and start writing it all down because if I wait until the next morning, I often won't remember it all.

The other time I've found I hear Him often is when I go upstairs to take care of my children's rabbits or when I go up to put away their laundry.

It's kind of become a running joke between Shane and me because every night after I go up to feed the rabbits, I'll come downstairs with a profound word from God.

One of those nights, the Lord spoke to my heart so clearly, "Jenny, one of the biggest deceptions that Satan uses against my children is an *inability* to have self-reflection."

As I sat and prayed about this more, I realized He didn't say that there was a lack of desire to have self-reflection. He said there was an inability to have self-reflection.

In today's terms, I think a great word to use for this would be "denial." One definition that *The Oxford Pocket Dictionary of Current English* has for this word states, "failure to acknowledge an unacceptable truth or emotion or to admit it into consciousness, used as a defense mechanism."

In Greek, the word "denial" is the word *arneo*, which is "to deny, to disown, to reject, to refuse, or to renounce."

I like to break it down in the following way:

Inability to have self-reflection.

- to deny the truth
- to acknowledge the truth
- to disown the truth
- to reject the truth
- to refuse or renounce the truth

Not due to a lack of desire to change, but due to a conscious *ability* to do so.

There is only one way we can change. And that is if we acknowledge the truth about ourselves. As hard as that may be. As painful as that may be.

We all know that we cannot change what we won't acknowledge. If we stay in this state of denial living in this reality all our own, then we will never be able to have true self-reflection and true change and step into all of the promises God has planned for us.

We also must acknowledge the truth of God. His truth, not ours.

Once we can acknowledge the real truth about ourselves apart from Christ, the most beautiful gift He then gives us is that we can then exchange that ugly truth for His truth about us. The great exchange. That great exchange on the cross was not only for our eternal salvation, but it was also for our whole well-being in every aspect of our lives here on earth. But we cannot exchange what we cannot see, do not see, and do not acknowledge. And if we choose to stay in this inability of self-reflection, then we will never truly have all that God has for us.

We will block our blessings.

I am pretty sure you do not want to block your blessings, right?

If you find your prayers are only including all of the things that you want God to change about everyone else, you'd better just stop that right now and start asking God to give you the ability to see the things about yourself that you need to see so that you can surrender them to Him and allow Him to help you change them.

"But blessed [spiritually aware, and favored by God] are your eyes, because they see; and your ears, because they hear" (Matthew 13:16).

Satan uses this inability to have self-reflection in all of us. And God is the only one who can give us the ability to see the things in ourselves that we need to see. It is not our job to point out other people's flaws, nor is it their job to point out ours. We do have the responsibility to hold people accountable to God's Word, but we have to be so careful in how we handle that.

God is the one who deals with people and changes people.

It most likely will not be comfortable to discover all of the things you need to change, but in Scripture, it tells us to be excited for God's correction because that's a sign of His love.

Once you have these personal revelations, the next step will be your willingness to ask Him to help you change. Do not expect to be able to change yourself; that job is reserved for Him through Christ and the Holy Spirit.

One example comes to mind. I have a friend, and I love her dearly. She is beautiful, smart, and talented, and she loves the Lord.

I don't hear from her that often, but when I do, it is usually when she is in a time of personal crisis or when she needs some words of encouragement, which I am happy to give.

I have noticed that she will always ask me for advice or input, and because she asks, I will give it. Always being careful to give her advice that lines up with the Word, of course, because I know that the Word of God works and can help her. Every time I've given her this input, her response has always been, "Oh, I know; I've already done that." Or, "Oh yes, I know; I already tried that."

So basically, she already knows everything about everything, and she's already doing all the things, yet she is not doing well; she is depressed; she is frustrated and sad, and she calls for advice.

I believe that my friend is deceived by the inability to have self-reflection. She has a desire, but she is spiritually blinded. She cannot see and cannot hear what God wants her to see and hear, and therefore she is unable to have the change she desires to have. There is a pride problem. And where there is a pride problem, God cannot work the way He wants to work.

One other example to give you, I have been a health and wellness coach for a long time. And with all humility, I am really good at what I do, not because of me but because God has gifted me in that area.

I cannot even count how many people have come to me for help over the years, and when we talk and I begin to give them suggestions on what they can work on and change in this area of their life, I'm amazed at some of the responses:

Response 1: "Oh, I've already tried all of that; it didn't work."

Response 2: "Oh, I want to feel better, but I'm not giving up my Coke."

Response 3: "Oh yes, I already know what to do, and I have done it, but it just doesn't seem to work for me."

Can any of you relate to this? They want help and have a desire and need to change, but they really believe that they already know all there is to know, they've already done all there is to do, and really, they just want someone to sympathize with them while they complain. This tells me that they are not ready for true change; because if they were, those responses would never even be a thought in their minds. They would show up and be ready to do whatever they need to do and listen with open ears to make the changes they need to make.

And then, as if all of this wasn't difficult enough to do, the next step is that you have to stick with it. And keep going. And stick with it some more. For how long, you ask? Until.

The truth is, none of us have arrived, and we never will. All of this is an ongoing process, and we must be intentionally asking and seeking within ourselves and working with the Holy Spirit rather than blaming, complaining, murmuring, and sitting in self-pity. Where has wallowing and self-pity really ever gotten us in life anyways? All that does is keep us exactly where Satan is counting on us to stay.

Here are some practical steps for you to follow so that you have the ability to have self-reflection:

1. Pray for God to reveal all of the things about yourself that need to change, not so you can feel condemned and terrible about yourself, but so that you can confess them and take them to Him.

2. Once those things are revealed, repent and exchange those ways or things for His way. (Don't expect it all to happen overnight, commit to the process and stick with it.)

3. Continue to work with God to break all of the strongholds, habits, and ungodliness off of your life.

# Chapter 21

## Supernatural Living

Do you believe your Bible? I mean, do you really believe your Bible in its entirety? We all must realize that we can't just pick and choose certain scriptures that we like and then just ignore the scriptures we don't care for. We have to realize that we have to read, meditate on, and receive the Bible in its entirety. Not to be taken out of context or misused, but to be used for our benefit and used for us to see God and His will more clearly.

For example, we all love to hear scriptures about supernatural abundance, love, peace, prosperity, and God's promises for us. I've never been in a room where the crowd hasn't gotten up and shouted when someone is talking about the resurrection and our forever home in heaven. Hallelujah!

But let me tell you, I've also been in rooms where someone mentions the scriptures about tithing and giving, talking in tongues, or doing things God asks us to do, even when we don't feel like it, out of obedience to Him, and there is no one to be found standing up and shouting for that!

Seriously think about it!

I don't know about you, but I want to step into the supernatural living that Jesus died for me to have. I am eternally and whole-heartedly grateful and thankful for my salvation and my ability to go straight to my Father through the Son anytime. But my goodness, Jesus didn't suffer and die for us for only that reason!

He died so we could have supernatural health. Supernatural provision. Supernatural protection. Supernatural blessings.

And I want that! Don't you? So, if the Bible tells us we are loved and accepted and perfected in Christ, then that's something to celebrate, but also, if the Bible tells us to tithe and give and that there is a supernatural law of reaping and sewing, well then that is something to celebrate as well.

If the Bible tells me I'm favored and loved, then I am favored and loved! Step into that, friends; step into that way of living. Don't focus on what this world says. Don't focus on what this world does. And for goodness' sake, do not worry about pleasing people so much that you never step into these promises that God has for you!

Focus. What do you focus on? What are you spending your time and energy focusing on?

I have a story from the Bible to share that relates to focus, and I believe it can truly change your life.

In the book of Matthew, there is a story of a miraculous feeding of five thousand men, as well as women and children. Jesus took the five loaves of bread, and two fish, blessed them, and they multiplied, and then the disciples took the food and fed all of the people. It says everyone was satisfied and that the disciples then picked up twelve baskets full of extras.

We often focus on the miracle of this story because it was an amazing miracle and example of grace and love, but have you ever thought about how much work that must have taken for the disciples? Twelve men feeding five thousand men, as well as women and children. Possibly twenty thousand people the twelve disciples fed and served that day. And then, after feeding everyone, they went around and picked up all of the leftovers, put them into the baskets, and carried them. That sounds pretty tiring as well.

Let's talk about what happens next. It is late at night, they've just witnessed a complete miracle, but physically they are tired. Jesus then tells them to get into a boat. He did not ask them if they wanted to get into the boat; He directed them to get into the boat. And then Jesus knowingly pushed them out into the water into a storm. Jesus then left and went up on the mountain by Himself to pray, and guess where the disciples were? They were out on the boat in the middle of a storm. The Scripture says that wind and waves tossed and battered the boat.

So just to clarify, the disciples are tired and worn out, it is late at night, it is dark, and Jesus has intentionally sent them out onto a boat in the middle of a storm and left them there.

Then it states that sometime between 3 a.m. and 6 a.m., the disciples noticed something out on the water. They could not quite make out what it was; it states, at first, they thought it was a ghost. Since they couldn't make out who it was, that tells us that Jesus was far enough away that they could not recognize Him, and let us not forget they were in the middle of a storm.

Then Jesus speaks out to them and tells them, "Take courage; it is I! Do not be afraid!"

Peter cries out and says, "Lord, if it is You, command me to come to You on the water."

Jesus said, "Come!"

In the initial moments Peter was on the water, his focus was on Jesus. Steadfast and focused. The Scripture then tells us that Peter saw the effects of the wind and that he was frightened and so he started to sink and cried out, "Lord, save me."

But look at the next part: Immediately, Jesus extended His hand and caught him, saying to him, "O you of little faith, why did you doubt?"

You see, when Peter was focused on Jesus, he was walking on the water. And based on the fact that it states Jesus was far enough away that they couldn't recognize Him, yet when Peter fell, Jesus *immediately* reached out and caught him; I would say Peter walked on the water for some time before he started to sink.

It was not until he lost his focus and saw the wind that he started to sink. He lost his focus on Jesus.

This story teaches us that when we focus on Jesus, we can do miraculous things, but when we lose our focus on Him and start to focus on everything else, we sink.

And what was the reason Jesus pushed them out into the storm anyway? He sent them across because on the other side was a city full of people that needed healing. Because they went across the water, through the storm, and got through to the other side, all who were sick there came and were healed.

If you aren't truly happy in life, ask yourself, "Where is my focus?" That simple question may reveal a lot to you and show you what you can change.

Jesus said, in John 15:18, "If the world hates you [and it does], know that it has hated Me before it hated you."

You need to realize that you are not here to please people. If living a supernatural life is of interest to you, you really need to leave the people-pleasing desire behind you and press into living to please God.

Let's take a little inventory here of our commitment to God and making Him first place in our lives. And trust me when I say I'm taking the inventory right along with you.

Write your answer right next to these questions, and then ask yourself what it is you can do better and how you plan to do so.

1. How often do you read your Bible?

2. How much do you tithe or give?

3. Are there areas of your life where you compromise what's right?

4. How much do you talk with God?

5. How much time do you spend with God?

6. Do your emotions dictate your life?

7. Do your thoughts dictate your actions?

8. Do your results in life make you angry at God?

9. Do you take credit for your victories in life?

10. Do you seek out things in order to gain people's approval?

Just to make sure everyone understands, this is not to condemn any of us; this is to get us to see areas that we need to improve in and work with God in so that we can receive the supernatural living and life God has for us.

# Chapter 22

## Victors and Victims

I believe victory is something we decide. Being delivered from habits and circumstances is God's desire for us, sure, but it's our decision.

And I believe that what enables us and leads us to those decisions is hunger. You need to be hungry for God. Not for stuff, not for status, or any of that stuff I spoke of earlier. You need to be hungry for God. He has to be first place in your life.

If you want to go to the next level in life, then you need to decide to go to the next level with God.

We have all been victims in this life, in one way or another, or what the world would call victims. And we get to decide if we will stay and sit in that, or if we will go with God and go through it, overcome it, and then use it for good.

A victor is someone who's gone through and then turns around and helps those that are still trying to make it through.

That's what this book is for. I have been through some stuff in my forty-four years on this earth.

Sexually abused by the time I was three and then through most of my childhood. Emotionally, physically, and mentally mistreated as I was growing up. Witness to countless episodes of dysfunction and mental illness. Disappointment, heartbreak, bad choices, homelessness, lack, hopelessness. I also know many of you have been through way worse.

As crazy as it sounds, we would not be able to help others who are going through hard times if we have never been through hard times ourselves.

This life is not all about us. This life is about God and serving others, and God will always get us through, get us to the other side and then use us to help other people.

God does not work alone; He works through people. Will you allow Him to work through you?

Will you choose to be a victor and not a victim?

I hope that you will because your life is special. Your life is worth sharing, and your story is needed. You are needed.

# Chapter 23

## Seasons

I've shared some of my stories with people over the years. And most times, when they hear the profound miracles that God did for me, they look at me awestruck, and some have even said things like, "Well, God hasn't shown up like that for me."

Here is what I have learned in my own walk with God. He shows up in different ways at different times, but one thing is certain for those who are born again, He will always show up.

When God gave me the "billboard" on the sidewalk that day, He did so because that was a season that I was in, and God knew that I needed that profound message in a profound way to stay strong. Although I've heard from Him in other ways since then, I can honestly say that He's never given me a billboard quite like that since that day. He will meet us in our season and show up in the way He knows that we need Him to show up. What we have to do is make sure that our hearts are right. What I mean by that is you know your performance is imperfect, but you have the deep desire to follow Him and be like Him; you love Him, and you really do want to please Him. Those are things that we need to do to have a heart for God.

If you read about David, his performance was not perfect. He was a warrior for Christ, but his behavior was not perfect. Yet God calls David a man after His own heart.

That's because David humbled himself before the Lord; even

in his imperfections, he did have a desire for God.

As we grow and mature spiritually, God will show up in different ways than He did when we were baby Christians. The more we mature spiritually, the more responsibly we have to stay steadfast with God even when the billboards don't show up.

The day I got my billboard, I was hungry and eager for God, but I was a spiritual baby. So God met me in that season and gave me profound miracles because just as I was after Him, He was also after me, and He knew that I needed those things in that season in order to stay on track with His plans for me.

These days, I don't get billboards, and sometimes I don't even feel like God is there with me. But spiritual maturity is the ability to live past what we feel and stay steadfast in what we know to be true. Of course God shows up; it's just that He shows up differently as I am in a different season.

I even remember one day in prayer, asking God why I hadn't gotten any more billboards from Him. I felt Him speak to my heart, "Jenny, look around you. Everything you see is your billboard that I am here, and of my goodness."

If you need a reminder of God's goodness, just look around you. Study the plants and the animals. Watch them. Study the seasons and the way everything works and comes together so perfectly. Get to a place of spiritual maturity where you own and control your emotions, and they do not own and control you. Get to a place where what you know overrides how you feel.

That, my friends, will ensure that you always have peace.

What season are you in when it comes to your spiritual maturity? God is there. He will not leave you nor forsake you. Just come to Him as you are and commit to your relationship with Him.

One thing is for sure; life is full of seasons. You will go through seasons of maturity as you grow, but God's favor is not for only one season or another; His favor is for a lifetime, according to Psalm 30! As you grow with Him, He's going to take you from one glory to another to another. His greatest blessing and victories for you are not in your yesterdays; they are in your tomorrows! Amen!

Awaken your great faith and stir up what is already in you through Christ! Get up! Keep going! Stand up! Believe!

Speaking of seasons, you do realize that all of us will have an ending season here on this earth, right?

The one thing we can all agree on is that, at some point, we will all die. Our bodies will perish and be disposed of, but it is our spirit that will live on.

Earlier in this book, I asked you, "What are you doing with this life that God gave you?"

Decide today to make it better, not to settle for good or okay, but to create a great life and to work with God to do so. And when you get there, don't forget how it felt when you were just starting or where you were during your journey. Don't forget to reach back and help the others who are trying to get there too!

Your life is important. You are important. You matter. You are special, and you do have a purpose here.

It does not matter what's happened to you, what you've done, what someone said about you, or even what you believe about yourself.

The only thing that matters is what God says about you. Who He says you are in Him. What He's already finished for you on the cross, and the love that He has for you.

So, you get to decide. Are you going to pursue God and His

will for your life?

Or are you going to keep doing things your way?

Are you going to stay stubborn and stuck in your thoughts, your feelings, your desires, your habits, and your mediocrity? How is that working for you anyway?

No matter what you choose, God is chasing you. He's with you down every road, up every mountain; He's the wind in the trees, the still small voice in your heart. God is always pursuing you, just waiting for you to do the same.

Can you hear His echoes?

The End

# Afterword

I hope this book has blessed you and your life.

Thank you, TBN, for the opportunity to share my story and God's love.

And thank You to my loving, good, generous Father in heaven for the gifts You've given me and for Your strength, courage, and wisdom to share them in order to glorify You and help Your children. My prayer is that people will never be focused on me but that they will only focus on Your goodness and pursuit of them.

# About the Author: Some Fun Facts about Jenny

Shane and I launched our ministry in 2023, Cheesecake and Conversation. (If you love homemade cheesecake, jump over and order one of his! His tagline is "With one bite, all things are possible!")

We would love for you to stop by our Facebook and Instagram and would love to have you tune into our podcast, which you can locate on all major podcast platforms. (*Cheesecake and Conversation with the Bishops.*)

If you would like for us to come to speak in your community, please click on the booking link located in our bios via our social media pages.

I am one hundred percent a jock at heart, having been an athlete all my life. In the early 2000s, I was a professional wrestler, and by 2011 I had become a professional physique athlete.

For over two decades, I have served hundreds of clients as a personal trainer and nutritionist. Just like God teaches us about getting to root causes and planting good seeds, I believe the same applies to our health and wellness. Although I have programs and help for everyone of all fitness levels via an online portal, I do specialize in helping women who struggle with slow metabolism and not being able to drop body fat and keep it off.

You will find my wellness platforms at @jennybwellness on Instagram, TikTok, and Facebook.

Please stop by the link https://msha.ke/jennybwellness to learn about all the ways I can serve you!

I am also an autoimmune warrior who, by the grace and guidance of the Holy Spirit, is pharmaceutical-free, and I have learned to manage and overcome this health struggle through proper nutrition, supplementation, and God's goodness. We all need to be declaring the finished works in our health in Jesus' name.

Due to my extensive resume over the years as a sought-out trainer, gym owner, and entrepreneur, I also have been blessed enough to have a business coaching program available specifically for personal trainers or gym owners who wish to expand their businesses and serve more clients. More details about that at jennybishop.com as well.

I also love DIY, home renovation and remodeling, as well as doing anything creative!

I love writing, music, and the outdoors.

CPSIA information can be obtained
at www.ICGtesting.com
Printed in the USA
LVHW051939140723
752119LV00012B/684